THE BOOK OF LISTS

BY

JUSTIN RICHARDS AND ANDREW MARTIN

BBC BOOKS

Published by BBC Books,
an imprint of BBC Worldwide Publishing
BBC Worldwide Ltd, Woodlands, 80 Wood Lane
London W12 0TT

First published 1997
ISBN 0 563 40569 4

Printed and bound in Great Britain by Mackays of Chatham
Cover printed by Belmont Press Ltd, Northampton

INTRODUCTION

'I'll start by making out some lists' — *Jo Grant,* **Terror of the Autons**

Welcome to **Doctor Who – The Book of Lists** which, not surprisingly, consists of a couple of hundred lists. The initial concept for this began in a fanzine called *Stock Footage* about thirteen years ago, but little of what appeared there has survived to form part of this book (mercifully). All the research for this has been done more or less from scratch, if only to check our wonky memories. This endeavour would be enough to put normal people off **Doctor Who** forever. Hasn't had much effect on us, however.

This book is aimed at **Doctor Who** fans, trivia buffs, people looking for something out of the ordinary to leave in the toilet, and those sad individuals who spend time compiling questions for the local pub's trivia quiz. It covers **Doctor Who** as televised, from the very first episode up to and including the BBC/Universal television film (which we refer to as **Doctor Who: The Movie**). While we may make mention occasionally of related productions like the **K-9 and Company** television special and the two cinema films starring Peter Cushing, we do not treat anything other than the **Doctor Who** TV series as 'canonical'. And we don't include the Children in Need special **Dimensions in Time** in that canon (though we may mention it from time to time).

It is also worth noting that the lists are not necessarily exhaustive – for example, in our list of hot beverages featured in **Doctor Who**, we may well have omitted a couple of sequences (by accident or design). Our objective for this volume has been to entertain rather than to slavishly enumerate. And part of the entertainment, of course, is in spotting the omissions! Lists with a relatively low, finite number of entries (actors to have appeared with most of the Doctors, for example) we have of course striven to make definitive, exhaustive, and correct. Doesn't mean we've managed though.

Acknowledgements

We'd like to thank the following people who didn't specifically request us not to – Peter Anghelides, Gary Russell (who suggested the idea for a book like this many years ago), and the DumbleCon and *Black and White Guardian* guys (for a certain general ethos).

Anyone we have inadvertently or otherwise neglected to mention here should (a) be thankful we have spared their blushes and/or (b) cadge a free copy of this book as recompense.

Justin & Andrew
December 1996

PRODUCTION

SPLENDID FELLOWS, ALL OF THEM
ACTORS WHO HAVE APPEARED WITH LOTS OF DOCTORS

Actors who have appeared with every Doctor

No one! As the American pilot only featured two British actors, in the lead role, there was little opportunity for people who had previously appeared in the series (who were, naturally, almost exclusively British or members of British Equity) to show up again. But here are the artists who have appeared with the most Doctors. And note that we have not included the Valeyard as a bona fide Doctor, or counted appearances alongside flashbacks or still photographs.

Actors who appeared with seven Doctors

John Scott Martin
> *He was a Dalek operator with Doctors 1-7, plus assorted other speaking and non-speaking parts, beginning with a Zarbi in* **The Web Planet***.*

Roy Skelton
> *Roy provided Dalek voices with Doctors 2-7, plus Monoid (***The Ark***) and Cyberman (***The Tenth Planet***) voices for the First Doctor. Additionally he appeared in minor roles including Norton in* **Colony in Space***, James in* **The Green Death***, and Marshal Chedaki in* **The Android Invasion***.*

Anthony Ainley
> *As the Master, he appeared with Patrick Troughton, Jon Pertwee and Richard Hurndall in* **The Five Doctors***, and also performed some standard Mastery against Tom Baker, Peter Davison, Colin Baker and Sylvester McCoy to bump up his total.*

Actors who appeared with six Doctors

Nicholas Courtney
> *He played space security agent Bret Vyon in* **The Dalek Master Plan***, then began his long-running appearances as Alistair Gordon Lethbridge-Stewart in* **The Web of Fear***. Originally a Colonel, from his second appearance (***The Invasion***) onwards a, or rather 'the' Brigadier. Never appeared with the Sixth Doctor, except in the Children in Need 'special'* **Dimensions in Time***.*

Jay McGrath
> *An extra who appeared in* **The Reign of Terror***, then with Jon Pertwee, Tom*

Baker, Peter Davison, and with Colin Baker and Patrick Troughton together in **The Two Doctors.**

Pat Gorman

Pat appeared mainly as an extra or walk-on, occasionally upgraded to minor speaking roles. First cast as a non-speaking rebel in **The Dalek Invasion of Earth**, *and made regular appearances until* **Attack of the Cybermen** *where, as well as a man in the Telos work party, he made one of several appearances over the years as a Cyberman.*

Les Conrad

A walk-on and extra from **The Dalek Invasion of Earth** *to* **Vengeance on Varos.**

John Leeson

Although he actually appeared only in a scene with Elisabeth Sladen in **The Five Doctors**, *strictly speaking that added Patrick Troughton, Jon Pertwee, Peter Davison and Richard Hurndell to his appearances with Tom Baker. He then went on to appear with Sylvester McCoy, as a voice artist on* **Remembrance of the Daleks.**

David Banks

Was a Cyber Leader with Peter Davison, and with Troughton, Pertwee and Hurndall in **The Five Doctors**, *then Colin Baker and Sylvester McCoy in* **Attack of the Cybermen** *and* **Silver Nemesis.**

Tony Starr

An extra and Dalek operator. He may have actually appeared with seven Doctors — there is an extra credited in BBC documentation for **Dalek Cutaway** *as Tony Starn. This could be a spelling error or even an earlier version of his name. Otherwise, first credited on* **The Underwater Menace**, *last credited on* **Remembrance of the Daleks.**

Graham Cole

Appeared as an extra with Tom Baker, Peter Davison and Colin Baker, and also with Troughton, Pertwee and Hurndall in **The Five Doctors**. *First worked on the aborted* **Shada**, *then* **The Leisure Hive**. *Last appeared in* **The Twin Dilemma** *before joining the cast of* **The Bill.**

Leslie Weekes

Yet another non-speaking performer, with a pedigree stretching from **Dalek Cutaway** *to* **The Trial of a Time Lord.**

3

ONE MAN IN HIS TIME
ACTORS WHO HAVE APPEARED IN THE MOST STORIES AS DIFFERENT CHARACTERS

Strictly speaking *characters* such as Daleks and Cybermen are different individuals in different stories – they must be as they are usually killed off! However, this list is limited to recognisably different characters, and also omits non-speaking roles (which would naturally tend to dominate things).

Pat Gorman
> Not counting his many extra and walk-on appearances, he has played 15 minor parts, credited on-screen, from a Cyberman in **The Invasion** through to a Cyberman in **Attack of the Cybermen.** He has also appeared in various UNIT ranks – a corporal in **Invasion of the Dinosaurs** and an unspecified 'soldier' in the next UNIT story Planet of the Spiders. His moments of glory must be when he played three roles in one story – Colonist, IMC guard, and Primitive in **Colony in Space**.

Terry Walsh
> Thirteen roles, not counting numerous non-speaking appearances as a stuntman, including regular doubling for Jon Pertwee and Tom Baker. He was also a fight arranger on numerous stories. His first credit was as a stunt-Auton in **Terror of the Autons**, his last as Doran getting thrown to **The Creature from the Pit**.

Roy Skelton
> Counting his Dalek and Cybermen voices as one role each, he has played ten parts, half of them voice only. His actual appearances include the invisible Spiridon Wester in **Planet of the Daleks** (well, he briefly becomes visible when he dies), and a short-notice fill-in role as Mr James in **The Green Death**.

Stuart Fell
> As well as numerous appearances as a stuntman and stunt double, he has played a total of nine credited roles. These include the body of Alpha Centauri in **The Curse of Peladon** and **The Monster of Peladon**, as well as the body of the Morbius monster in **The Brain of Morbius**. Slightly less bizarre, he was a fire-eating entertainer in **The Masque of Mandragora**.

John Scott Martin
> Eight roles, even counting all his 'appearances' as a Dalek operator as just one. As

'himself' his roles have included Hughes — the first victim of **The Green Death**, *and a security guard in* **Robot**.

Michael Wisher
*Seven roles, including that of Dalek voice artist. His most memorable creation was the original Davros, and in that story (***Genesis of the Daleks***) as in others, he contributed extra voices as well as his main character. Other notable roles have included Rex Farrel in* **Terror of the Autons**, *Kalik in* **Carnival of Monsters**, *and Morelli in* **Planet of Evil** *as well as another heavy make-up job to appear as Magrik in* **Revenge of the Cybermen**.

Dave Carter
Started off as an extra, but soon graduated to speaking parts in seven stories between 1970 and 1975. His biggest role was his last, as Grierson in **The Android Invasion**.

Michael Sheard
Six roles in six stories over 22 years. His first role was Rhos in **The Ark**, *his last was the Headmaster in* **Remembrance of the Daleks**. *He is best remembered, however, as Laurence Scarman in* **Pyramids of Mars**.

Peter Halliday
Appeared in six stories from Packer in **The Invasion** *to the Vicar in* **Remembrance of the Daleks**.

Walter Randall
Six roles between 1964-1974, starting with Tonila in **The Aztecs** *and finishing with a guard captain in* **Planet of the Spiders**. *All his other roles were for director Douglas Camfield, including most notably El Akir in* **The Crusade**.

Max Faulkner
Many appearances as stuntman, but has had six credited roles, culminating in Nesbin in **The Invasion of Time**.

Gerald Taylor
Six parts, even counting all his 'appearances' as a Dalek operator as one role... As himself, he plays Baker's Man in **The Daemons**.

Graham Leaman
Five roles between 1967 (the Controller in **The Macra Terror***) and 1973. He played Time Lords (the same Time Lord?) in both* **Colony in Space** *and* **The Three Doctors**.

Alan Rowe

*Played five roles, although two were in the same story (**The Moonbase**). He is best remembered for Edward of Wessex in **The Time Warrior** and Colonel Skinsale in **Horror of Fang Rock**.*

John Caesar

*Five speaking roles (from Man in Market in **The Romans** to a soldier in **Invasion of the Dinosaurs**), plus about as many non-speaking.*

Philip Madoc

*If you were to include his appearance in the film **Daleks – Invasion Earth 2150AD** that would make five roles. In this instance, we shall leave it up to your own conscience whether you treat the films as canonical! He is worth mentioning anyway for his powerful performances as the War Lord in **The War Games**, and Solon in **The Brain of Morbius**.*

WHAT'S IN A NAME?
PRODUCTION PSEUDONYMS

Writers' pseudonyms

These are generally credits used when there has been some dispute between writers and production team, or when substantial editing or rewriting has been necessary for technical reasons and the original writer was unable or unwilling to perform the task.

The Dominators by Norman Ashby

A much-altered script by Mervyn Haisman and Henry Lincoln, which lost an episode along the way.

The Daemons by Guy Leopold

*A name used to disguise the fact that producer Barry Letts was co-writing a story with playwright Robert Sloman. Sloman went on to contribute three adventures under his own name, while Letts wrote several **Who** radio serials.*

Pyramids of Mars by Stephen Harris

Illness and other commitments prevented Lewis Greifer from rewriting his own original story when it was found to be unworkable, and so script editor Robert Holmes began more or less from scratch, albeit on a similar theme.

The Brain of Morbius by Robin Bland

Subject of a familiar convention story, Robert Holmes once more rewrote a submission, this time by Terrance Dicks who had once been script editor to him as a freelance writer. Dicks, who was on holiday at this critical time, merely stipulated that the story go out under 'some bland pseudonym.'

The Invasion of Time and **City of Death** by David Agnew

*Not only is this the only pseudonym to be used more than once, the mythical Mr Agnew has also contributed to other productions, including **Target** and **Play for Today**, being a stock BBC drama pseudonym. The only link in **Doctor Who** terms is in producer Graham Williams, who co-wrote **The Invasion of Time** with script editor Anthony Read after a David Weir story fell through, then collaborated with Read's successor Douglas Adams on **City of Death**, which does bear a vague resemblance to the David Fisher script it replaced.*

Actors' pseudonyms

We are not concerned here with the real names of actors, but with names billed in Radio Times or on screen to conceal the identity of the actor playing a particular character and avoid spoiling the plot suspense.

🚂 'Sydney Wilson' as Koquillion – **The Rescue**

*To conceal the fact that this was in fact the character Bennett in disguise, this pseudonym was concocted from the names of the then BBC Head of Drama, Sydney Newman, and his Head of Series and Serials, Donald Wilson, who had had overall responsibility for the creation of **Doctor Who**.*

🚂 'Neil Toynay' as the Portreeve – **Castrovalva**

The first of two occasions when one of the Master's fiendish disguises was concealed by billing his alter ego with an anagram of 'Tony Ainley' playing the part.

🚂 'Leon Ny Taiy' as Kalid – **Time-Flight**

The second of these occasions.

🚂 'James Stoker' as Sir Gilles – **The King's Demons**

A twist on the previous ploy (since they had presumably run out of even semi-plausible anagrams of Ainley), Radio Times billed Anthony Ainley in this way on his next appearance: James Stoker being an anagram of Master's Joke. Sir Gilles' surname was Estram, an anagram of Master.

🚂 'Roy Tromelly' as the Dalek Emperor – **Remembrance of the Daleks**

This anagram concealed actor Terry Molloy's name, otherwise fans might have realised the fact that the Emperor was the latest incarnation of Davros.

Character pseudonyms

And lastly, the converse situation, where the name of a *character* might give away their surprise appearance or reveal a plot twist.

🚂 Alien (played by Steve Peters) – **The Seeds of Death**

The return of the Ice Warriors was disguised by this billing, while his superior Ice Lord was merely billed as Slaar. Peters and Bennion had not previously appeared as Ice Warriors, so the actors' names were no clue.

🚂 Melkur (played by Geoffrey Beevers) – **The Keeper of Traken**

Melkur was in fact the Master's TARDIS, albeit uniquely played by an actor. As a clue to the outcome of the story, the character played by Anthony Ainley, who is absorbed by the Master, is named Tremas – again, an anagram.

The Unknown (played by Gareth Milne) – **Black Orchid**

> To hide the plot revelation that the scarred relic in the attic is the brother of Charles Cranleigh, **Radio Times** and part one's end credits billed his character enigmatically.

The Renegade (played by Ian Collier) – **Arc of Infinity**

> Replacing Stephen Thorne who had created the role in **The Three Doctors**, Collier appeared as Gallifreyan pioneer Omega, suitably renamed to preserve the mystery.

Icthar, Scibus, Tarpok, Sauvix – **Warriors of the Deep**

> Confusingly, given that the rest of the cast have similarly unlikely names, the Silurian and Sea Devil leaders are billed by individual names here. The original serials featuring the creatures made do with calling their counterparts Old Silurian, Young Silurian, Silurian Scientist, and Chief Sea Devil, which is a lot easier to follow. Whether they were actually trying to disguise who they were, or merely out to confuse, is anyone's guess.

The King (played by Gerald Flood) – **The King's Demons**

> This of course is Kamelion rather than bad King John, but is billed in this way to keep the pretence up. Curiously, he's still billed as the King on the end of part two, when the cat's out of the bag.

Grenville/Enzu played by Tony Scoggo – **The Trial of a Time Lord (parts nine to twelve)**

> The only time a single character has been credited with two names, neither of which is his own. This character was first credited as Grenville, his cover name. In the next episode the same actor was billed as Enzu, his pseudonym when he is disguised as a Mogarian. When he is killed the Doctor gives his 'real' name as Hallett.

ARE WE YET TO COME?
STORIES MADE OUT OF SEQUENCE

For various reasons, **Doctor Who** stories were not always recorded in the order in which they were transmitted. Out-of-order production did not begin to occur until the 1970s, when programmes were made sufficiently far in advance of transmission for production teams to have any choice in the matter. The instances of out-of-sequence story recording are:

The Daleks episode 1

As the videotape for the original version turned out to be faulty, this episode had to be re-recorded from scratch after episodes 2 and 3. The only sequence surviving from the original version is the recap at the start of episode 2, which was film telerecorded for that purpose, and so was not faulty. This means that the very first appearance of a Dalek, at the end of episode 1, is not the first Dalek footage to be recorded.

The Curse of Peladon and **The Sea Devils**

*These were recorded in reverse order with the result that the latter story and the season opener, **Day of the Daleks**, both Earth-based, could be separated by an alien planet story, while **The Sea Devils** could take advantage of better weather earlier in the year for its extensive location filming.*

The Three Doctors, Carnival of Monsters and **Frontier in Space**

*The Three Doctors was recorded after both of these stories. This both fitted in with Patrick Troughton's other commitments and allowed William Hartnell more time to prepare himself for the rigours of performing. Matters were further complicated regarding **Frontier in Space**, as the end of episode six was deemed unsatisfactory, and was re-recorded as part of **Planet of the Daleks**, allowing in addition direct continuity between the interlocking serials. To cap it all, episodes five and six of **Frontier in Space** were recorded in reverse order.*

The Ark in Space, The Sontaran Experiment, Genesis of the Daleks and **Revenge of the Cybermen**

*As the new production team were keen to get away from the format of two four-part and three six-part serials for the 12th series, they used the location recording facility for one potential six-parter as a two-part all-location story, with the studio allocation given over to an all-studio four-part production. Thus **The Sontaran Experiment** was the first story to be made entirely on location, sharing most of its production crew with **The Ark in Space**. That story, as a further cost-saving measure, had its main*

10

sets reused in **Revenge of the Cybermen**, which, partly to avoid storage costs and damage, was recorded next. **Genesis of the Daleks** followed.

Planet of Evil and Pyramids of Mars

These were reversed in production order – possibly to separate **Pyramids** from the season opener, **Terror of the Zygons**, another Earth-based story.

Horror of Fang Rock, The Invisible Enemy, Image of the Fendahl and The Sun Makers

The Invisible Enemy was always to have been the second story in the season, but was recorded first when Terrance Dicks' story **The Vampire Mutations** (also known as **The Witch Lords**) was cancelled because it would coincide with the BBC's prestige production of **Dracula**. Dicks thus had to come up with a speedy replacement, and switching the production order gave him more time. **Image of the Fendahl** and **The Sun Makers** may again have been swapped to avoid two similar-feel stories going out in succession, although this caused problems as Leela's old costume had to be re-introduced at the end of **Image** to explain its reappearance in **The Sun Makers**.

Destiny of the Daleks, City of Death and The Creature from the Pit

These were recorded in reverse order, so in fact **City of Death** was recorded and transmitted second.

Meglos, Full Circle and State of Decay

State of Decay was perhaps recorded first because incoming producer John Nathan-Turner favoured allowing new characters a chance to find their feet before recording their debut story. In this case, the new companion Adric was also allowed further breathing space while **Meglos** was recorded, before making his 'first' appearance in **Full Circle**.

Castrovalva, Four to Doomsday, Kinda and The Visitation

Peter Davison's first story as the Doctor was recorded fourth in the 19th series. **Four to Doomsday** was taped first, followed by **The Visitation**, then **Kinda**.

Arc of Infinity and Snakedance

Arc, which began the 20th series, was recorded after the second story in the season, **Snakedance**.

The Mark of the Rani and The Two Doctors

These were recorded the other way round, the latter having moved intended location during its planning stages from America to Spain.

The Trial of a Time Lord (parts nine to twelve) and The Trial of a Time Lord (parts thirteen to fourteen)

*Assuming you count these as separate stories... As with **The Sontaran Experiment** and **The Ark in Space**, the last two segments of the **Trial of a Time Lord** sequence were virtually the studio and location work for one story. The 'Vervoid' section was studio bound, while the final two episodes were made first, mostly on location, although all the trial room material was recorded in one block.*

The Happiness Patrol, Silver Nemesis and The Greatest Show in the Galaxy

*These were intended to have been shown in recording order, but the BBC's Olympic coverage meant that transmission of the season's first story, **Remembrance of the Daleks**, was pushed back. As part one of **Silver Nemesis**, the anniversary story, had been made to go out on the 23rd November, it was necessary to swap **Happiness Patrol** and **Greatest Show**. This precipitated an unfortunate continuity error, as Ace's jacket sports an earring in **Happiness Patrol** and **Silver Nemesis** which she doesn't obtain until **Greatest Show**.*

The 26th season

*This season, consisting of **Battlefield**, **Ghost Light**, **The Curse of Fenric** and **Survival** has the distinction of being the only season of **Doctor Who** transmitted completely out of recording order. It was actually made in the order **The Curse of Fenric**, **Battlefield**, **Survival**, **Ghost Light**.*

BACK FOR MORE

COMPANIONS (AND DOCTORS) WHO PLAYED OTHER ROLES IN THE SERIES

This refers to bona fide other roles – not doubles, android copies, clones and the like.

▰ Peter Purves (Steven Taylor 1965-66)

> *After failing an audition to be a Menoptra in **The Web Planet**, Purves was cast as cowboy-hatted Texan innocent Morton Dill in **The Chase**. This led to him being cast as new regular Steven Taylor, starting in the final episode of the same serial.*

▰ Nicholas Courtney (Colonel/Brigadier Lethbridge-Stewart 1968-1989)

> *After being considered for the part of Richard the Lionheart in **The Crusade**, the same director, Douglas Camfield, cast Courtney as Bret Vyon in **The Daleks' Master Plan**, a character killed off after four episodes. In 1968, Courtney was offered the part of Captain Knight in **The Web of Fear** (also destined for death), but was promoted to Colonel when first choice David Langton backed out of the Lethbridge-Stewart part.*

▰ Jean Marsh (Sara Kingdom 1965/66)

> *Although only appearing in one story, Sara is usually considered as companion as she made several voyages in the TARDIS. Jean Marsh had previously appeared in **The Crusade** as Richard the Lionheart's sister Joanna, and returned to the programme in 1989 as Morgaine in **Battlefield**.*

▰ Jacqueline Hill (Barbara Wright 1963-65)

> *After leaving the profession to bring up her children, Jacqueline Hill returned to acting in the late 70s and appeared as Lexa in 1980's **Meglos**.*

▰ John Levene (Corporal/Sergeant/RSM Benton 1968-1975)

> *John Levene originally worked as an extra, appearing in **The Moonbase** as one of the Cyberman army. Shortly after this, he worked as a non-speaking desk constable in **Z Cars** for director Douglas Camfield, who then cast him as a Yeti in **The Web of Fear**. This then led to the part of Corporal Benton in Camfield's next Who story **The Invasion**. After returning as a Yeti in Patrick Troughton's last episode, Levene rejoined **Doctor Who** as part of the regular UNIT team in **The Ambassadors of Death**.*

13

Ian Marter (Harry Sullivan 1974/5)

Ian Marter auditioned for the role of Captain Mike Yates in 1970, and was remembered by producer/director Barry Letts, who cast him as naval officer John Andrews in **Carnival of Monsters**. *Letts again thought of square-jawed Marter when looking for someone to play Surgeon Lieutenant Harry Sullivan, a character devised to handle action sequences when it was thought an older, less active actor might replace Jon Pertwee.*

Lalla Ward (Romana mark 2 1979-81)

As with Peter Purves, Ward was cast as a regular immediately after her first appearance in the show (as Princess Astra in **The Armageddon Factor**). *Indeed, much play is made in her first broadcast story as Romana,* **Destiny of the Daleks** *of the resemblance, with the Doctor protesting that she can't go around wearing someone else's body (which has an ironic ring regarding Commander Maxil in* **Arc of Infinity** *— see Colin Baker below).*

John Leeson (Voice of K9 1977-79,80/81)

As K-9 didn't appear in the season 16 story **The Power of Kroll**, *Leeson was cast as long-suffering refinery worker Dugeen. In a sense, his earliest connection with the series was as a BBC announcer voicing trailers for, among countless other things,* **Doctor Who**. *He later re-created this role, as well as providing some of the Dalek voices, in* **Remembrance of the Daleks**.

Colin Baker (the Doctor 1984-86)

Baker was nearly cast as Jellicoe by Christopher Barry for **Robot.** *After appearing in* **Blake's 7** *in 1980, he was offered the role of Commander Maxil in* **Arc of Infinity**, *who at one point shoots the Doctor. The clip of this was aired on BBC news programmes when it was announced that he was to become the Sixth Doctor.*

ACTION TRANSFERS
ACTORS APPEARING A LOT, BUT NEVER FOR THE SAME DIRECTOR

Must be nice to be wanted – if only once! Strictly speaking, we should include Jackie Lane as Dodo, Caroline John as Liz Shaw, and Lalla Ward as Romana (discounting the clip of her from Shada used in The Five Doctors) – all count as well. But as regulars, the director of a particular story would not have had the choice.

Michael Sheard
> *Each of his six roles was for a different director: Michael Imison, Timothy Combe, Paddy Russell, Derrick Goodwin, Fiona Cumming and Andrew Morgan.*

Dallas Cavell
> *Five parts, for Henric Hirsch, Douglas Camfield, Hugh David, Michael Ferguson and Fiona Cumming.*

Graham Leaman
> *Again five roles, for John Davies, Hugh David, Michael Ferguson, Michael Briant and Lennie Mayne.*

John Abineri
> *Worked for Hugh David, Michael Ferguson, Michael Briant and Norman Stewart.*

Cyril Shaps
> *Employed by Morris Barry, Michael Ferguson, Barry Letts and Michael Hayes.*

John Woodnutt
> *Over eleven years was used by Derek Martinus, Paul Bernard, Douglas Camfield and John Black.*

WEARING SOMEONE ELSE'S BODY
CHARACTERS PLAYED BY DIFFERENT ACTORS (IN DIFFERENT STORIES)

In a series like **Doctor Who**, the number of characters who appear in heavy make-up or enveloping costumes makes it far easier to substitute one actor for another if required. It is sometimes necessary to make a substitution if the original actor is unavailable through work commitments, or more sadly, death. Then again, **Doctor Who** being the weird and wonderful thing it is, there are sometimes other reasons...

- Doctor Who/the Doctor
  Of course, the prime example is the series' lead character...

- The First Doctor
  *When making the anniversary story **The Five Doctors** in 1983, the production team were faced with the problem that William Hartnell had sadly died in 1975. To overcome this obstacle, actor Richard Hurndall re-created the part.*

- The Master
  *Roger Delgado was killed in a car accident in 1973, and when it was decided to bring back the character he had personified in **The Deadly Assassin**, the production team decided to make their Master very different – a scarred, degenerate figure at the end of his natural lifespan. In that instance, Peter Pratt provided what was mainly a vocal performance. When the Master was resurrected once more, as **The Keeper of Traken**, Geoffrey Beevers was cast as a similarly disfigured version of the Time Lord, who then regenerated into the Delgado-esque aspect of Anthony Ainley. Eric Roberts took over the role for **Doctor Who: The Movie**, when the viscous and vicious spirit that was all that remained of the executed Master took over the body of a San Franciscan ambulance driver.*

- Romana
  *As well as being played by Mary Tamm (**The Ribos Operation** to **The Armageddon Factor**), and Lalla Ward (**Destiny of the Daleks** to **Warriors' Gate**), three other actresses played the intermediate bodies of Romana in **Destiny**: Maggy Armitage, Yvonne Gallagher and Lee Richards.*

- Borusa
  *Once the Doctor's tutor, the wily Borusa rose to the eventual presidency of Gallifrey's High Council of Time Lords. First played by Angus Mackay (**The***

16

Deadly Assassin), in **The Invasion of Time** *he was portrayed by John Arnatt, in* **Arc of Infinity** *by Leonard Sachs, and finally, in* **The Five Doctors**, *by Philip Latham.*

Davros

Originally portrayed by Michael Wisher in **Genesis of the Daleks**. *Wisher was unavailable in 1979 when the character returned in* **Destiny of the Daleks**, *and David Gooderson assumed the part. The next three appearances of Davros featured Terry Molloy* — **Resurrection of the Daleks**, **Revelation of the Daleks** *and* **Remembrance of the Daleks**.

The Silurian Scientist/Tarpok

Although somewhat obliquely referred to, it is implied that the character of Tarpok in **Warriors of the Deep** *was intended to represent the same creature as the Silurian scientist in the original* **Doctor Who and the Silurians**, *despite the fact that he looks radically different, his voice has completely changed, and his third eye just flashes when he speaks, rather than opening doors, killing people and performing other handy functions. The original character was played by Pat Gorman, with voice, as with all the Silurians in that story, by Peter Halliday. Tarpok was portrayed by Norman Comer, who provided his own voice.*

The 'Planetarians'

The epic story **The Daleks' Master Plan** *was preceded by a one-episode filler story called* **Dalek Cutaway**. *Several alien delegates were featured aside from the Daleks, and played mainly by extras. When these reappeared in episodes of the main serial some months later, all were recast, to avoid retainer payments. The only speaking aliens featured were Trantis, played by an extra in* **Dalek Cutaway** *but by actor Roy Evans in* **Master Plan**, *and Malpha, who was first played by Robert Cartland, but in his reappearance the role was taken by Bryan Mosley (*Coronation Street*'s Alf Roberts).*

Corporal Palmer

A 'stock' UNIT corporal played, for example, by Denys Palmer in **The Three Doctors** *(credited as 'Palmer') and by Bernard G High in* **Terror of the Zygons** *(credited as 'Corporal'). Unless, of course, they are intended to be different people...*

TWO TIME LORDS?
DOUBLES FOR THE DOCTOR — AND OTHER ODDITIES

Doubles generally fall into two categories, whether they are substituting for a lead actor or anyone else. There are those who are look-alikes, and there are stunt doubles.

- Brian Proudfoot – **The Reign of Terror, The Space Museum**

  *In the first case, Proudfoot doubled for William Hartnell in the series' first ever location filming. As the Doctor was only to be seen in long shot roaming through the 'French' countryside, it was simpler to use a double than to drag Hartnell out on a Sunday morning (the usual time for such filming). In **The Space Museum**, Proudfoot was used in a sequence where the Doctor was required to look at himself and his companions in their own future, preserved in a glass case.*

- Edmund Warwick – **The Dalek Invasion of Earth, The Chase**

  *Having apeared in **The Keys of Marinus** as the scientist Darrius, Warwick, who bore some resemblance to Hartnell, was required to step in at the last minute and double for him when he was slightly injured while recording **The Dalek Invasion of Earth**. Warwick spent episode 4 of the story 'unconscious'. Then, when Terry Nation's script for **The Chase** required the Doctor and his companions to be threatened by a robot double of the Doctor, Warwick was cast again. This role required several complicated, and not entirely successful, sequences where he both played the robot, and the Doctor, as required. Hartnell was used for all close-ups, but there are several medium shots used where Warwick is all-too recognisable.*

- Albert Ward – **The Romans, The Celestial Toymaker, The Smugglers**

  *Not really cast as a double in the usual sense, Ward only ever doubled for Hartnell's hands. His digits doubled for Hartnell's in a film insert of burning plans in **The Romans**. In **Celestial Toymaker**, the Doctor is made mute and invisible apart from his hand (again allowing Hartnell a holiday), while in **The Smugglers**, Ward's hands appeared in a sequence involving a card game against the pirate Jamaica (Elroy Josephs).*

- Gordon Craig – **The Smugglers, The Tenth Planet**

  *Craig was used in **The Smugglers** for a film sequence involving the Doctor being rowed to the smugglers' ship. **The Tenth Planet** was actually recorded as the first* story of a new recording block, and Hartnell's contract had expired at the end of the previous block. Hartnell came back on a one-off basis to do this story, and as he was unwell, a double was used for the pre-filming of the TARDIS crew crossing from the ship to the entrance to Snowcap base. As the plot did not require the Doctor in episode 3 either, Hartnell had a week off, and Craig is seen collapsing at the start of the episode, and later asleep in bed – the collapse transpiring to be the first sign that the Doctor is about to regenerate.

Peter Diamond – **The Enemy of the World**
All the regulars were doubled for in film sequences in this story, apart from in close-up, as they were required for the rigours of studio recording the previous story, and stuntman Peter Diamond doubled for Patrick Troughton here. This story also featured a double of the Doctor, Salamander. Some shots used a crude split-screen process, but the climactic event of Salamander being sucked out of the TARDIS in-flight was performed by Diamond.

Mike Smith – **Fury from the Deep**
In a nominal sense, as he piloted the helicopter seen in this story, when it was supposed to be being flown by the Doctor. And no, it's not that Mike Smith – just someone else with the same name who also flies helicopters.

Chris Jeffries – **The Wheel in Space, The Dominators**
*Jeffries substituted for Troughton in **Wheel in Space** episode 2, when the Doctor is knocked out (holiday-for-the-Doctor-time again), and during filming on location for **The Dominators** (which despite starting a new season on air, was recorded immediately after **Wheel**).*

Tommy Laird – **The Seeds of Death**
In episode four, the Doctor has once more been knocked out, and spends time lying on a bunk while all around him fight Ice Warriors. Extra Laird stood (or rather lay) in for Troughton.

Terry Walsh – Jon Pertwee and Tom Baker eras (1970-79)
*In too many stories to enumerate here, Terry Walsh was the regular stunt double for Jon Pertwee. He is most noticeable in **The Monster of Peladon** when it is obviously he who is fighting the rebel miner Ettis at the end of part four. Walsh continued as a stuntman into the Tom Baker era, notably doubling for him in **The Sontaran Experiment** after Baker broke his collar bone.*

Unnamed sailor – **The Sea Devils**
Allegedly, a sequence was filmed with the Doctor and Jo abseiling down a cliff for this story, but didn't make it to the final cut. Doubling for both artistes were Royal Navy

abseiling experts, part of the generous facilities provided for this story.

Stuart Fell – The Masque of Mandragora

A little too short really to pass for Tom Baker, but it is Fell doing various stunts around Portmeirion.

David Rolfe, Roy Seeley, Derek Chafer – The Leisure Hive

Once again not doubles in any usual sense, these extras played parts of the Doctor's body in the scene where he appeared to be ripped apart by the Recreation Generator.

Derek Chafer, Mike Handley, Ridgewell Hawkes, David Rolfe, Roy Seeley, Jeff Wayne – The Leisure Hive

And again... in the sequence in part four of this story were the Doctor turns out to have been duplicated numerous times, but clothed as Pangol, these extras played his doubles.

Adrian Gibbs – Logopolis

An honorary mention here for the actor who played the Watcher, the Doctor's spooky premonition-in-humanoid-form, up to the moment where he merges with Tom Baker's Doctor and is revealed to be Peter Davison.

Gareth Milne – Warriors of the Deep

The first time Peter Davison's Doctor was required to do any serious stunt work, Milne took on the task of plunging over a guard rail into a disguised swimming bath.

Bill Weston – The Mark of the Rani

Doubled for Colin Baker for the really dangerous stunts. The rest, Baker insisted on doing himself.

Geoffrey Hughes – The Trial of a Time Lord

In a warped kind of sense, Mr Popplewick is a double for the Valeyard, who is really the Doctor – but Popplewick is in fact a disguise... this is getting confusing!

Mike Tucker – Dragonfire

Visual effects assistant who stood in for Sylvester McCoy's feet in video effects shot of the Doctor's POV looking down into the ice chasm.

Tip Tipping – Remembrance of the Daleks, Survival

*Performed the sequence in **Remembrance** of the Doctor sliding down a cable on his umbrella to the top of the Dalek shuttle craft, as well as various other stunt performances, most notably the part of Corporal Tipping, who is duffed up by the traitorous Mike Smith (no – it's still not that Mike Smith, nor is it the one who flies helicopters). In **Survival** Tipping and stunt rider Eddie Kidd performed the 'chicken run' sequence near the end of the story, doubling respectively for McCoy and Will Barton (Midge).*

- Paul Heasman – **Silver Nemesis**
  Fell in the river for Sylvester McCoy in part one.

- Unknown – **Doctor Who: The Movie**
  Someone must have doubled for Paul McGann in the various high-risk stunt sequences – the insurance company wouldn't have had it otherwise!

Other oddities

Here are some instances of people playing a Doctor who wasn't the *real* one at the time:

- William Hartnell and Patrick Troughton – **The Three Doctors**
  Not really what you'd describe as doubles in any real sense, but they weren't the genuine article at the time.

- Richard Hurndall, Patrick Troughton and Jon Pertwee – **The Five Doctors**
  Same situation in almost every way. Tom Baker appeared only as an insert from **Shada**.

- Patrick Troughton – **The Two Doctors**
  Just couldn't stay away...

- Michael Jayston – **The Trial of a Time Lord**
  As the Doctor's twelve-and-a-halfth regeneration.

- Sylvester McCoy – **Time and the Rani**
  Briefly doubled for his predecessor in the pre-title regeneration sequence.

HAM-FISTED BUN VENDORS
PEOPLE WHO HAVE PLAYED JO GRANT

One close to our hearts, though we couldn't explain why. Perhaps it's the thought of Stuart Fell in a flared white trouser-suit that does it.

- Katy Manning
  The standard model.

- Mildred Brown
  When Jo is aged close to death in The Claws of Axos, the redoubtable Mildred took over for the really wrinkly bits.

- Stuart Fell
  The afore-mentioned trouser-suit sequence, doubling for Jo as she clambers up into the sea-fort after Terry Walsh's Doctor in **The Sea Devils**.

- An unnamed sailor
  In, of course, **The Sea Devils** *(see Doubles for the Doctor, above).*

- Linda Regan
  Later minor star of **Hi-De-Hi***, stood in for Katy in some of* **Carnival of Monsters***.*

TWO PEAS IN A POD
DOUBLES FOR OTHER COMPANIONS

Companion doubles tend to be either for stunts or location filming. This list, to make life easier, includes people who have played a companion without actually being the person supposed to be playing them (like Kate O'Mara's imitation of Bonnie Langford as the Rani pretends to be Mel in **Time and the Rani**).

Billy Cornelius – **The Aztecs**
Head swathed in exotic head-dress, Cornelius doubled for Ian in his filmed fight with Ixta (himself doubled by David Anderson).

Peter Diamond (?) – **The Dalek Invasion of Earth**
Documentation is not available on who doubled for Ian falling out of a doorway well above ground level in this story, but someone did – best guess is Diamond, who is credited as stunt arranger on the story.

Viktors Ritelis – **The Crusade**
Production assistant (floor manager) on this medieval tale, Ritelis bravely volunteered to have his arm smeared with honey and let ants crawl over it when William Russell (Ian) declined to. And who can blame him?

David Newman and Barbara Joss – **The Chase**
Doubled for Ian and Vicki in a location long-shot sequence on the planet Aridius.

May Warden – **The Daleks' Master Plan**
Played 'Old Sara', i.e. when Sara Kingdom is aged to death by the Daleks' Time Destructor, Ms Warden was substituted for Jean Marsh in a film sequence to show her grisly end.

John Clifford – **The Massacre of St. Bartholomew's Eve**
Doubled for Peter Purves in a studio film sequence, as Purves had to carry the bulk of the adventure and so was not available for pre-filming as well.

Peter Pocock – **The Tenth Planet**
Stunt double for Ben in sequence of Cutler trying prevent him from sabotaging the Z Bomb rocket (Michael Craze was nursing a broken nose).

Richard Hallifax and Sarah Lisemore – **The Enemy of the World**
Alongside Peter Diamond's Doctor, these two doubled for Jamie and Victoria messing about on an 'Australian' beach at Littlehampton.

Maurice Brooks – **The Web of Fear**
Not really a regular (in the televisual sense) at this stage, but it would be churlish to omit the extra whose feet provided the first glimpse of Colonel Lethbridge-Stewart in

episode 2 of this story. As the character did not appear properly until episode 3, expense was spared by hiring someone else to lurk in the shadows.

Ken Gibson – **The Wheel in Space**
Probably doubled for Jamie, although the available documentation is not clear.

Richard Hallifax – **The Mind Robber**
On his own this time, but doubling for Jamie again, albeit briefly. Shots of Fraser Hines in episode 2 were recorded later and edited in, as Hines had chicken pox and had to miss the studio session.

Hamish Wilson – **The Mind Robber**
Perhaps the best-known substitution. As Fraser Hines had chicken pox, Wilson stood in for Fraser Hines for most of episode 2 and part of episode 3.

Unknown – **The Ambassadors of Death**
Someone doubled for Liz Shaw (wearing her big hat) for sequences of her driving Bessie on real roads in episode 3. Caroline John had not passed her driving test at the time, and so all shots of her obviously driving had to be filmed on the customary disused airfield. The stunt of falling over the weir was performed by Caroline John herself, despite the fact that she was pregnant.

Walter Henry – **Inferno**
Henry played the Primord created by the infection of Platoon Under Leader Benton in most scenes. John Levene did the actual transformation sequence and some close-ups (both on film), but it was easier to have someone else play his Primord self in the studio. Oddly, the other Primords were played by different, upgraded extras to those who had played the technicians they had mutated from.

Darren Plant – **The Time Monster**
Played Baby Benton.

Terry Walsh – **The Sontaran Experiment**
Doubled for Harry and the Doctor, aas well as playing Zake, and fight arranging.

Unknown stunt performer – **Genesis of the Daleks**
Fell off the gantry for Sarah.

Jennie le Fre – **The Brain of Morbius**
Performed Sarah's stunt fall down the stairs towards Solon's house guest's room.

Stuart Fell – **The Talons of Weng-Chiang**
Doubled for Leela jumping out of Litefoot's window.

Roberta Gibbs – **The Stones of Blood, The Androids of Tara**
Doubled for Mary Tamm as Romana in tricky cliff-clinging and horse-riding situations. Despite being a 'double' story, all scenes requiring two Mary Tamms in **Androids** *were actually achieved with split screens.*

24

Maggy Armitage, Yvonne Gallagher, Lee Richards – **Destiny of the Daleks**

> *Played the dry-run possible bodies demonstrated by Romana before she settled on the Princess Astra look.*

Sue Crosland – **Destiny of the Daleks**

> *Fell down a shaft in the Kaled city to save Lalla Ward the bother.*

Susie Brown – **K-9 and Company: A Girl's Best Friend**

> *If you choose to count this, she doubled for Sarah.*

Vanessa Paine – **Black Orchid**

> *Again a 'double' story, but this time someone was required to stand in for Sarah Sutton in some sequences, both as Nyssa and her mirror image (give or take a mole), Ann Talbot.*

Nick Gillard – **Mawdryn Undead**

> *Stunt double for Mark Strickson as Turlough in the hazardous crashing-a-vintage-car sequence.*

Sian Pattenden and Lucy Baker – **Mawdryn Undead**

> *Later in the same story, Tegan and Nyssa start de-ageing rapidly. Interesting to note that Tegan didn't have an Australian accent as a child.*

Richard Sheekey – **Mawdryn Undead**

> *Played the 'other' Brigadier in the scene where the two aspects meet.*

Ellie Bertram – **Paradise Towers**

> *Doubled for Mel as she struggles with the pool cleaner robot.*

Tracey Eddon – **Remembrance of the Daleks, The Curse of Fenric**

> *Jumping through schoolroom windows, and clambering down the outside of churches in place of Sophie Aldred.*

Tip Tipping – **Remembrance of the Daleks**

> *A touch of (albeit traditional) cross-dressing, doubling for Ace as stunt-driver of the 'detector van'.*

Ken Barker (probably) – **Battlefield**

> *Got blown through a wall for Nicholas Courtney – all in a day's work.*

TOOLS LIKE THESE

Pity the poor visual effects designers on **Doctor Who** – faced with tiny budgets and little time to complete their work. There are occasions when the inspired thing, or even the only thing possible in the circumstances seems to be to grab anything lying around and adapt it to create the required highly sophisticated machine the script calls for. It may well be that 90% of the time this is done so well you can't spot it – however there are times when the careful viewer may notice such oddities as:

- Lava lamps
  *Stuck at the back of the set in **The Wheel in Space**. They also feature as sophisticated Dalek machinery in the film **Doctor Who and the Daleks**.*

- Lightning globe
  ***Remembrance of the Daleks**' time controller whotsit, unfortunately quite noticeable as the latest in executive toys.*

- Pen on a cord
  *Everyone was wearing them in the late 70s, including various characters in **The Armageddon Factor**, who seemed to think they were communicators. Apparently this was an on-the-spot decision in the studio when someone realised they'd be needing communicators.*

- Bicycle reflector
  *Transport had obviously moved on (as it does) in Kaldor City, so those waste-not want-not dudes in **Robots of Death** decided to use them as 'corpse markers' aka 'robot deactivation discs'. In the same story, the robots' hands are covered by Marigold rubber gloves.*

- Cricket gloves
  *The Android in **The Visitation** wears them.*

- TV remote control
  *Obviously a slightly advanced version of the traditional device, used by Morgus in **The Caves of Androzani**.*

- Calculator
  ***Underworld** sees the Minyans using slim, metallic models as little gadgets aboard their spaceship. Perhaps they were supposed to be calculators?*

- Trendy 70s coat stand
  *Horrid, chromium plated thing with big rings dangling off it. In **Planet of the Daleks**, the Daleks courteously leave one outside the Doctor and Codal's cell, with Codal's gun belt hanging on it. Another of these objects is seen in **The Deadly***

Assassin in the Time Lord robing room.

Music cassette box

Also in **Planet of the Daleks**, *the TARDIS log is just a cassette box with a few bits and pieces glued to it to make it look complicated and technical.*

Practice golf balls and flexible pipes

The Moonbase *and* **Tomb of the Cybermen** *Cybermen swore by these as their external 'skeletons' – a shame no one ever ripped those tubes off a Cyberman and swung it around to make that annoying 'whooping' noise!*

Wet suits

To the Cybermen in **The Wheel in Space** *and* **The Invasion** *they were the height of fashion. By* **Earthshock**, *the Cybermen are reduced to wearing flightsuits, moon boots and ski gloves.*

Lorry hub-caps

Strewn around the Kaled city in **Destiny of the Daleks**, *and attached to the base of the Jaggaroth ship in* **City of Death**.

Sink plughole

Emits the jet of freezing gas in **The Faceless Ones**. *Then again, perhaps it's easier to nip down the DIY shop than go all the way back up into space because you've forgotten a bit of alien equipment?*

Gas cooker igniter

One of those hand-held gadgets they used to have for lighting your gas burners plays the part of the rocket (suspiciously closely-cropped on screen) that is fired at the TARDIS at the beginning of **The Armageddon Factor**.

Spray cream cans

Cleaned up with wire wool, they served as Ace's Nitro-9 canisters.

Plastic pill packaging

Not used itself, but photographed and blown-up for the walls in the 60's TARDIS set (it was also the model for the 3- dimensional walls).

Sink plungers and car (originally Mini) indicator lights

No clues!

Police box

OK, so it was never a real one, let's not get picky.

NOT A JOT

Typically, a **Doctor Who** script editor had already written for the series when appointed to the post. Many wrote stories during their own tenure, for one reason or another, and having left the post many were pleased to make later contributions. However, one or two have escaped ever being credited with writing for **Doctor Who**, although all of course did some writing while they were editors.

Donald Tosh

> *Just about qualifies, at a pinch, as he is credited as co-writer of the last episode of his last story, **The Massacre of St. Bartholomew's Eve**, with the story's proper author, John Lucarotti. Tosh's main input was the closing scene, which introduces new companion Dodo Chaplet. While it is not unusual for story/script editors to write such scenes, it is for them to receive credit, which may indicate in this case that Tosh had left by this point. In any case, his contribution was not a story as such.*

Peter Bryant

> *One of only two people to be credited both as story editor and producer on **Doctor Who** (the other being his successor Derrick Sherwin), Bryant was also credited as associate producer (on **The Faceless Ones**), but never as writer.*

Antony Root

> *Spent very little time working on the programme, and is credited on only three stories, **Four to Doomsday, The Visitation** and **Earthshock**. The writer he edited on **The Visitation**, Eric Saward, was then appointed to take over what was only a stop-gap post for Root, although he returned to cast an eye over Saward's scripts of **Earthshock**, neatly avoiding Saward appearing to commission himself. Saward and Root share the script editor credit on **K9 and Company: A Girl's Best Friend**.*

Andrew Cartmel

> *Script editor on all of Sylvester McCoy's stories except the first (**Time and the Rani**). He has since written several **Doctor Who** novels, but has never contributed a script.*

SPIN-OFF PRODUCTIONS

Television

Apart from numerous spoofs and sketches, there are few bona fide spin-offs. A series following the fortunes of Victorian adventurers Jago and Litefoot (from **The Talons of Weng-Chiang)** came to nothing, nor did a mooted series about UNIT which might have prefigured **The X-Files**. Most famously, Terry Nation tried to get an American television series about the adventures of the Daleks off the ground in the late 60s, again without success. Here are some more successful (if sometimes dubious) tv spin-offs.

🔹 **K-9 and Company: A Girl's Best Friend**

Acknowledging the popularity of the character K-9, but declining to have him/it in **Doctor Who** *any longer, the BBC produced this pilot for a possible series between series 18 and 19. Popular companion Sarah Jane Smith was brought back, but the episode was no great shakes, and no series followed. The set-up was continued however by Sarah and K-9's appearance together in* **The Five Doctors**.

🔹 **A Fix with the Sontarans (Jim'll Fix It)**

As a 'Fix' for a young **Doctor Who** *fan in the long-running wish-fulfilment series, Eric Saward wrote this short, not-very-serious adventure which was shown on the 23rd March 1985, in an edition following episode two of The Two Doctors. Colin Baker starred, with Janet Fielding as Tegan, and Clinton Greyn and Tim Raynham as Sontarans.*

🔹 **Serendipity**

Stretching the point a bit, but... Immediately after leaving **Doctor Who**, *Katy Manning presented this arts and crafts series made by the BBC's further education department. Not really a spin-off in the usual sense, but its title recalled the catch-word in Manning's last story, where the serendipity of her knocking fungus onto a sample of maggot slime provided the clue as to the cure for* **The Green Death***. As a series,* **Serendipity** *gives a unique sociological insight into 70s fashion – groovy!*

🔹 **Moonbase 3**

In a sense, as it's the only programme (other than K-9 and Company) made by a **Doctor Who** *production team in their spare time (ha ha) between series of* **Doctor Who***.*

🔹 **Dimensions in Time**

Well, it's difficult to see what else it was...

Radio

Radio became, briefly, one way of carrying on BBC-made Doctor Who during its 1985/86 hiatus and after the cancellation in 1989. There have been some other programmes of note as well.

Who Was Susan Foreman?
> *One of a series of programmes on Radio 4 in 1996, catching up with the later adventures of characters in popular fiction.*

The Time Machine
> *An educational broadcast in 1976, with Tom Baker, Elisabeth Sladen and John Westbrook.*

Slipback
> *Written by Eric Saward, and consisting of six short episodes, this was broadcast as part of a strand called Pirate Radio 4. As this was on FM only, only those regions of the country which could receive such transmissions of Radio 4 at the time heard it.*

The Paradise of Death
> *Bringing back Jon Pertwee's Doctor, in the first of two stories broadcast in the 1990s. Script was by former producer, Barry Letts. Elisabeth Sladen and Nicholas Courtney re-created their old roles.*

The Ghosts of N-Space
> *The follow up, much delayed in transmission, and which was actually issued as a tape by the BBC first. The same team wrote and starred.*

Film

In the wake of 50s remakes of tv science fiction such as the first two **Quatermass** stories, **The Creature** and **The Trollenberg Terror**, came two colour films usually referred to as the Amicus films (even though they weren't made by that company, just by some of the same people who ran it). Plans for a third film based on **The Chase** were never followed-up, and nor was Disney's proposed film of **Marco Polo**. Tom Baker tried to get **Doctor Who and Scratchman** made in the mid Seventies, with Vincent Price as the villain and a script by Baker and Ian Marter. Most recently, Lumiere failed to get a film made before their rights expired. Jon Pertwee has said that while playing the Doctor he turned down various offers of **Who** films, not wishing to be still associated with the part by them after he chose to leave it.

◣ **Doctor Who and the Daleks**

> *Based on the television serial **The Daleks**, and starring Peter Cushing, Roy Castle, Jennie Linden and Roberta Tovey.*

◣ **Daleks – Invasion Earth 2150 AD**

> *Follow-up based on **The Dalek Invasion of Earth**. Here, Ian and Barbara were replaced by Bernard Cribbins' policeman Tom Campbell and Jill Curzon as Doctor Who's niece Louise.*

Records

A very small category, featuring only one true spin-off, called **Doctor Who and the Pescatons**. Issued by Arco Records in 1976, this featured Tom Baker and Elisabeth Sladen, and was written by Victor Pemberton. Other **Doctor Who** records have been edited versions of tv stories (**The Dalek Invasion of Earth**, **The Chase** episode 6 and **Genesis of the Daleks**) or compilations of music and sound effects. In the 1990s, several 1960s stories which either do not exist or only partly exist in visual form were compiled from off-air audio recordings made by fans.

Novels

Aside from the plethora of novelisations of tv stories published by Target, W.H. Allen and Virgin over the years, covering all but a handful of adventures, there has been established since the early 1990s a range of original novels from Virgin Publishing, the *New Adventures*. These carried the adventures of the Seventh Doctor onward, firstly accompanied by Ace, then by new companions. Written in the main by televised story writers and fans of the programme, they finished in 1997, to be succeeded by a range of novels featuring the Eighth Doctor, this time from BBC Books. Virgin also published a range called *Missing Adventures*, featuring older Doctors, and ostensibly fitting into gaps between televised stories. Again, this idea has been picked up by BBC Books.

Comics

A natural comic-strip character, it might be thought, the Doctor has featured in strip form almost since the series began, in publications such as *TV Comic, Countdown, TV Action* and latterly, *Doctor Who Weekly* – continuing to date in its successors *Doctor Who Monthly* and *Doctor Who Magazine*. There was also in the 1960s a strip featuring the Daleks alone, published in full colour in the comic *TV*

Century 21, otherwise mostly concerned with Gerry Anderson's output. Following **Doctor Who: The Movie**, *Radio Times* ran a comic strip featuring the Eighth Doctor.

Stage Plays

Only three, spread over the years. **The Curse of the Daleks** (by David Whitaker and Terry Nation) cashed in on sixties' Dalekmania and did not include the Doctor or any of his companions. **Doctor Who and the Daleks – Seven Keys to Doomsday** (by Terrance Dicks) in the mid seventies had Trevor Martin as the Doctor, the Daleks again providing some of the villainy. **Doctor Who – The Ultimate Adventure** (again by Terrance Dicks) starred Jon Pertwee and later Colin Baker (and for one night David Banks) as the Doctor. This time he was pitted against various horrors including Daleks, Cybermen, and some excruciatingly embarrassing songs.

Others

As well as the range of spin-offs produced by the BBC and other professional organisations, there have been a number of semi-professional and amateur extensions of the series, including tons of fan fiction in fanzines. Worthy of specific mention are the video productions **War Time, Downtime** and **Shakedown**, featuring companions and monsters rather than Doctors, and the Audiovisuals series of sound productions. A series of videos entitled **The Stranger** has also been produced, not **Doctor Who** productions as such, but produced by fans of the show featuring almost all of the (then) surviving lead actors and many 'companion' actors.

I DENY THIS REALITY
BITS OF STUDIO EQUIPMENT APPEARING IN SHOT

By accident

This was not that unusual in the early years of the show when recording was done 'as 'live', and retakes were only made where absolutely necessary. Nonetheless accidents do happen even in more recent times. Here are some examples from throughout the programme's history.

Microphone booms in shot

*In **100,000 BC**, a microphone boom pops into shot briefly at the top of the screen in the TARDIS interior scene. An outrageous example, in **City of Death**, occurs in one shot of the interview between Captain Tancredi and the Doctor in Renaissance Italy, where a microphone boom hangs above Tancredi's head, well in shot. When the same angle is cut back to shortly after, it has gone.*

Microphone boom shadows

*Microphone booms are the worst offender overall in this section, and their unscheduled appearances are legion – outstripped by a large factor by their shadows, which can be seen in pretty much every story made, albeit less and less as time goes on: nowadays it is often possible to remove them electronically. A good example of a boom shadow is in **The Time Monster** – moving over the TARDIS console as Jo wakes up on the floor of the console room.*

Unwanted reflections

*In **Inside the Spaceship**, a microphone boom is seen reflected in the TARDIS scanner, and bits of the studio are visible on tv screens in, among others, **The Space Pirates** and **The Three Doctors**. In the sequences with Cyril, Steven and Dodo in **The Celestial Toymaker** episode 4, a pedestal camera and sound boom are clearly reflected in one of the silvered walls. Slightly different, in the mind-assault sequence in **Death to the Daleks**, the Doctor's distorted face is achieved by shooting Jon Pertwee reflected in a sheet of flexible mirrorlon. When he moves away at the end of the sequence, the back of Pertwee's head is visible between the camera and the reflection.*

Cameras directly in shot

*A close-up of William Hartnell in **The Space Museum** episode 4 features a quickly-removed corner of a camera in the front of the shot. In **The Chase**, as well as a fleeting glimpse of something whizzing across the set in a high-angle shot of the Daleks' time machine interior, there is a crane-mounted camera in plain view at the back of the Mechanus jungle set* *in episode 5 of this story. Similarly in* **The Dominators**, *in a scene in the Dominators' ship in episode 3, a camera's zoom lens and pedestal are briefly in shot at the back of the set.*

Camera shadows
These are rarer, but there is one on Ian's back in **The Web Planet** *episode 2, and a really great one on Ben in the sick bay in* **The Moonbase**.

Kirby wires
Kirby wires themselves are often caught in vision, notably and most recently in **Timelash**. *In that case, when the Doctor and other descend into the eponymous time tunnel, the wires also manage to chafe flecks of polystyrene off the protruding 'crystals'. In* **The Tomb of the Cybermen**, *in scenes where Toberman is hoisted overhead by a Cybermen, the attachment device of his Kirby wire is visible.*

Visible radio microphones
As a way of avoiding boom shadows, sound supervisors can use radio microphones, if it is possible to fit them without the risk of picking up rustling from clothes etc. In **Terror of the Zygons** *there seemed an ideal opportunity to conceal the Zygons' microphones in the nodule just below their chins. Unfortunately in close-ups of Broton, the little grey mike is all too obvious.*

Things getting on camera lenses
There are other instances where cameras are visible, not in themselves but because things splash onto their lenses – one particularly noticeable example is in **Attack of the Cybermen** *when the Cyber Controller's green gunk hits the camera taking the shot towards the end of the story.*

On purpose

Now and again, bits of studio equipment or the studio itself can be seen, either as themselves or representing something else... ignoring, obviously, the studio floor!

Genesis of the Daleks
Where Davros' little microphone is what it seems...

The Seeds of Doom
A slight cheat, but the exterior of the World Ecology Bureau is really part of the exterior of TV Centre.

Warriors' Gate
Low-angle shots of the privateer corridors use the real studio lights (the roof being otherwise in darkness).

The Trial of a Time Lord
In the Hyperion III's hold, the real studio walls and stairways are used in vision.

HE WAS THE DOCTOR ALL THE TIME
UNRECOGNISABLE CAMEO APPEARANCES

Patrick Troughton, in the days before **Five** and **Two Doctors**, used to say that he'd like to return to **Doctor Who**, but uncredited, inside a monster costume. This is a list of people who have appeared in the series, some before they found fame, others who were already well-known, but you wouldn't know it was them unless you knew it was them...

- Peter Glaze – **The Sensorites**
  The Crackerjack stalwart was the Third Sensorite, the villainous City Administrator.

- Martin Jarvis – **The Web Planet**
  Before The Forsyte Saga made his name, Jarvis donned a Menoptra costume as Captain Hilio.

- Hywel Bennett – **The Chase**
  Not too heavily disguised, but awfully young, with silver make-up and peculiar head-adornment, as Rynian the Aridian.

- David Baron (Harold Pinter) – **The Abominable Snowmen**
  Using his stage name, the pausing playwright appears as Tibetan warrior monk Ralpachan in episodes 2-6, with lots of make-up and a big moustache.

- Bernard Bresslaw – **The Ice Warriors**
  Not exactly incognito, Bresslaw's well-publicised outing as what he thought was going to be a kind of Viking saw him encased in masses of fibreglass and latex.

- Stratford Johns – **Four to Doomsday**
  Again a not very discreet appearance, but caked in green make-up as Monarch, 'king of the frogs'.

- Christopher Wenner – **The Awakening**
  Maybe not a major star, but the former Blue Peter presenter made an appearance as the deformed man who bag-snatches from Tegan.

- Sarah Greene – **Attack of the Cybermen**
  Another Blue Peter presenter, in a role demanding the wearing of big silver head with distorting lenses. Alongside her for this treatment were impressionist Faith Brown, and since-then novelist Esther Freud, sister of Emma. Koo Stark backed out at the last minute...

EVERYTHING IN ENGLISH
USE OF SUBTITLES AND CAPTIONS

While there are many times when we could have wished for subtitles for the hard-of-understanding, there are only a few occasions when they have appeared for all to see. We do not include episode titles and production credits rolled over the action.

The Mind of Evil

> *The Doctor's exchange in Hokkien with Fu Peng is subtitled, all thanks to dialogue consultant, actress (Captain Chin Lee) and author's wife, Pik-Sen Lim.*

The Curse of Fenric

> *Russian dialogue early in part one is subtitled, before Sorin (in full Russian uniform and heavy accent) utters the immortal line, 'From now on, everything in English.'*

The Daleks' Master Plan

> *In the Christmas Day episode, **The Feast of Steven**, the silent movie chase sequence is blessed with inter-titles, that is, the dialogue captions traditionally used in pre-talkie days.*

The Deadly Assassin

> *Tom Baker's opening narration is also scrolled up on screen.*

Establishing captions

> *The only other thing approaching this is the use of establishing captions – such as 'Paris' (**The Reign of Terror**), 'Roma' (**The Romans**), 'Alastair Fergus' is given a caption when he appears on television (**The Daemons**), as does 'Alex MacIntosh' when he appears as a tv reporter of the same name in **Day of the Daleks**), 'South America 22nd November 1988' and 'Windsor, England 1638' (**Silver Nemesis**), 'Skaro' and 'San Francisco, 1999' (**Doctor Who: The Movie**).*

Ceefax

> *Last but not least, there is the non-narrative use of subtitles, that is, on Ceefax. These first appeared on **Warriors' Gate**, then on every story from **Black Orchid** onwards.*

NEVER THROW ANYTHING AWAY

Given the length of time Doctor Who has survived, it's hardly surprising that some sets, props, costumes and other bits and pieces have cropped up more than once. Here are just some of the things that have been reused, excluding of course things like the TARDIS prop and sets.

Sets

Aside from such stock items as the TARDIS, most sets are not kept because they are specific to one programme, and too bulky to store. However, some smaller items, such as bits of computer bank etc, can be retained. Also, sometimes sets are made from pre-formed material, which makes it hard to tell whether a set is new or reused.

- *Dalek equipment from **The Daleks** was reused in various Dalek stories during the Hartnell era of the programme.*

- ***The Keys of Marinus** – trellis-work walls and dividers turn up in episodes of this story in different places. Later they are reused in **The Romans**.*

- *The streets in **The Sensorites** are sets made for the city in **The Daleks**.*

- ***The Rescue** and **The Space Museum** both feature part of the spaceship set from **The Sensorites**. In the latter reuse it is incongruously part of the TARDIS interior.*

- *A cylindrical console with a perspex dome from **The Space Museum** turns up in **The Wheel in Space**. It is also in **The War Machines**, minus its dome.*

- *Eldred's space museum in **The Seeds of Death** reuses the drill from **The Dominators**, and, bizarrely, the astral map featured in the TARDIS in **The Web Planet** and **Galaxy 4**.*

- *Triangle patterned walls – first seen in **The Mutants**, have made many appearances, including **The Deadly Assassin**, **The Stones of Blood**, **Nightmare of Eden**, **The Horns of Nimon**, **Meglos**, **The Trial of a Time Lord** (parts one to four), **Dragonfire** etc.*

- *The sets of **The Ark in Space** were redressed and reused (to represent the same place) in **Revenge of the Cybermen**.*

- *Lattice walls, different from those in **Keys of Marinus**, first seen in **The Time Monster**, turn up again in **Death to the Daleks** in the Exxilon city.*

- Various control panels etc bought from Gerry Anderson's Century 21 Productions were used in **The Green Death, Time Warrior, The Ark in Space, Genesis of the Daleks, The Stones of Blood** and **The Armageddon Factor** among others.

- A chair from Solon's castle in **The Brain of Morbius** turns up in Madame Lamia's laboratory in **The Androids of Tara**.

- The spaceship interiors in **Delta and the Bannermen** and **Dragonfire** are the same set re-dressed.

- Tables used in **The Sensorites** reappear in **The Ice Warriors**. The matching chairs appear again in **The Space Museum**.

- The corridors of Marb Station in **The Trial of a Time Lord** (parts one to four), are reused as the corridors on Thoros Beta in **The Trial of a Time Lord** (parts five to eight).

- A set of small consoles with radar screens etc set in it are seen in a number of 1980s stories including **Terminus, Warriors of the Deep, The Twin Dilemma, Attack of the Cybermen,** and **The Two Doctors**.

Props (including visual effects)

- A Drahvin gun from **Galaxy 4** is used in **Genesis of the Daleks**.

- A plastic visor as worn by technicians in **The Ice Warriors** is used by Rago in **The Dominators**.

- An android skeleton from **The Android Invasion** is shackled next to Romana in the hyperspace ship in **The Stones of Blood**. In another cell is a Wirrn from **The Ark in Space**.

- The Gaztaks' guns in **Meglos** come from **The Pirate Planet, The Armageddon Factor** and **The Horns of Nimon**.

- Firearms from **The Pirate Planet, The Power of Kroll, Nightmare of Eden, The Horns of Nimon** and **Meglos** are used by the Fosters in **The Keeper of Traken**.

Costumes (including wigs)

- A spacesuit from **The Ambassadors of Death** is worn by a colonist in **Colony in Space**.

- Argolin wigs from **The Leisure Hive** crop up in **Time and the Rani** and **Dragonfire**.

- The back section of an Ice Warrior costume is used for one of Davros' 'pets' in **Genesis of the Daleks**.

- The troopers' helmets from **Earthshock** were worn again by the Train Guards in **The Trial of a Time Lord (parts one to four)**, and the Bannermen in **Delta and the Bannermen**.

- Crayford's spacesuit in **The Android Invasion** is a Thal one from **Planet of the Daleks**.

- The Gaztak costumes in **Meglos** come from various sources including **Carnival of Monsters** (Pletrac's robe), and the extras' headgear includes that worn by Graff Vynda K and Sholakh in **The Ribos Operation**. Another Gaztak hat turns up again in **Time and the Rani**, worn by one of the geniuses.

- Argolin robes from **The Leisure Hive** were re-dyed to be worn by the inhab-itants of **Logopolis**.

- A Terileptil mask from **The Visitation**, painted pink, is worn by a small alien extra in **The Trial of a Time Lord (parts five to eight)**.

- Extras' costumes in **Destiny of the Daleks** come from various stories including **Frontier in Space**, **Planet of Evil**, **The Robots of Death** and **The Pirate Planet**.

- A mutt from **The Mutants** turns up as Kriz in **The Brain of Morbius**, even played by the original actor, John Scott Martin.

- The spacesuits seen in **The Tenth Planet** are reused in **The Wheel in Space**.

Graphics

Logos etc are few and far between, and are seldom in a position to be reused, but there is one notable example, which is, as it turns out, rather unfortunate as it went on to become rather well-known:

- The Vogan logo in **Revenge of the Cybermen** is reused in **The Deadly Assassin** and ever since, up to and including **Doctor Who: The Movie**, as the familiar Gallifreyan circular emblem.

Material taken from other programmes

There are also occasions when **Doctor Who** has utilised settings and props from other programmes. Here are some notable examples:

- *The robot costumes in **The Mind Robber** were from a 1967 episode of **Out of the Unknown**, entitled **The Prophet**.*

- *The 'wheel' model in **The Wheel in Space** made a previous appearance in **Thirty Minute Theatre: The News Benders** earlier the same year, 1968.*

- ***The Seeds of Death** features a craft from **Out of the Unknown** and a spaceship seen in **Thirty Minute Theatre: The News Benders**.*

- *The Recovery 7 capsule in **The Ambassadors of Death** was 'shared' with the **Doomwatch** episode **Re-Entry Forbidden**.*

- *The spacesuits worn in **Invasion of the Dinosaurs** and **The Sontaran Experiment** were from the series **Moonbase 3**, made by the **Doctor Who** production team in 1973.*

- *The guards' helmets in **Frontios** originally belonged to Federation troopers in **Blake's 7**.*

NOTHING TO LOSE BUT YOUR CLAIMS
STORIES AFFECTED BY BBC STRIKES

For those of you born more recently than the early 70s, you probably won't remember strikes, but they were quite the rage a decade or so ago. The BBC was just as susceptible as any other organisation, and a number of stories were affected by them, with assorted results.

Spearhead from Space

A dispute over working with the larger sets being used in colour television meant that electronic studios were not available. This was circumvented by making the whole programme on film.

Doctor Who and the Silurians

The same dispute had a knock-on effect on the following adventure, when Barry Newbery's sets had to be adjusted to make them smaller than planned.

Robot

*A BBC scene shifters' strike in May 1974, midway through the first recording block for Tom Baker's first story. Recording had to be re-scheduled, but **Blue Peter** viewers got a sneak preview when the show came live from its intended studio, with the **Doctor Who** sets still in place.*

The Power of Kroll

Almost, but not quite... A strike blacked out transmissions of BBC programmes for the week preceding its scheduled broadcast. The dispute was settled just in time for most of that Saturday's programmes to go out as planned.

Shada

*The most notorious example, in this case a story was lost due to a strike breaking out part way through the recording of this six-part story in late 1979. Only one of three planned recording blocks was completed, plus some 'gallery' (electronic effects) work, and no substitute studio time could be found due to requirements for BBC Christmas programming. Incoming producer John Nathan-Turner tried to get extra recording time to complete the story as a 'special', but he had already won two more episodes for his first season, and it was not to be. The story finally saw some light of day, after a fashion, as part of **The Five Doctors**, and in 1992, as a BBC Video release with links by Tom Baker to fill the gaps in the recorded material.*

Enlightenment, The King's Demons and **Resurrection of the Daleks**

*A strike postponed recording on **Enlightenment**, which had several consequences. Re-scheduled recording meant that Peter Sallis and David Rhule, original casting for Striker and Mansell, were no longer available, and were replaced by Keith Barron* *and Leee John. The production was complicated already by the need for a remount of scenes from **Terminus** due to overrunning on that story. Recording of **The King's Demons** was affected too, and the delays meant that the planned recording dates for the original version of **Resurrection of the Daleks** were impinged upon. Rather than risking the anniversary story **The Five Doctors**, due to be taped immediately afterwards, it was decided to drop **Resurrection** and include it in the following series.*

Survival

A BBC pay strike meant that recording knocked off at 3pm on location for this story, but it did not have serious consequences for the completion of the story.

IDENTICAL, YES — THE SAME, NO

Errors occur in continuity even in feature films, as a consequence of shooting all the angles of a scene separately, and consecutive scenes on different days. Since early **Doctor Who** was mostly recorded continuously with several cameras, most errors occur between pre-filming and studio material. We have not included any differences in early episodes, between cliffhangers and their re-enactment the following week, but here are a few slip-ups to look out for:

The Web Planet
Different Menoptra masks were used in filming and electronic studio work.

The Chase
When the Doctor and Ian are in Frankenstein's laboratory, a Dalek can be seen in an alcove at the back of the set (from where it will later converse with the monster) – but at this point, the Daleks have not yet landed in the haunted house. When Frankenstein's monster emerges to do battle with the Daleks, it has mysteriously taken time to remove its bandages and dress itself. Also in this story, watch for the Doctor and his companions hurrying into the TARDIS, Daleks close behind on Aridius... How do they manage to get in through what seems to be the side of the police box (if that's the handle on the 'front')? Notice also the sudden change to daylight as a Dalek pitches into Ian's trap – it was night just a moment ago.

The Tomb of the Cybermen
The pitch of the Cybercontroller's voice changes drastically between episodes 2 and 3.

The Mind Robber
When Jamie attacks the redcoat at the start of episode 2, his sleeves are rolled up, but the cardboard cut-out he is turned into has its sleeves rolled down.

Doctor Who and the Silurians
When Dr Quinn enters the barn where the Doctor and Liz are in episode 3, his coat is wet from the rain outside. When we cut to him in close-up, and subsequently, he has dried off rather quickly.

Doctor Who and the Silurians
'Private' Wright has a Lance Corporal's stripe.

Inferno
Section Leader Elizabeth Shaw's hairdo in film sequences is different from that worn in the studio scenes.

The Claws of Axos
Stuntman Stuart Fell, playing a soldier, is shot by the Master's ray gun in episode two, and his beret comes off as he falls. Cutting to a different angle, the headgear has

reattached itself. In episode four, the Doctor appears to abandon Jo, UNIT and the others to their fate, leaving the Nuton power complex with the Master in the TARDIS. However, when the Axons break into the chamber shortly afterwards, the TARDIS can still be seen in one shot.

The Daemons

In the scene of Miss Hawthorne quelling the elements, her cloak bunches on top of her shoulders as she raises her arms. Cutting to the reverse angle as she turns to PC Groom, the cloak is fastened firmly in place around her shoulders. When the Doctor draws a circuit diagram on the windshield of his motorbike, he doesn't erase it before he drives off – but the next time we see him driving along, it has gone.

Frontier in Space

In episode four, when the Doctor enters the airlock of the Master's spaceship, he presses the right-hand of two buttons on the wall to open it. Later, when the Master is putting Jo in the airlock, he presses the left-hand button to open it. When the TARDIS is first seen in episode five, a side other than the door side is facing into the Master's control room. When Jo and the Doctor enter the ship at the end of the story, the door side has moved round, and is facing into the room.

Planet of the Daleks

Jo Grant's hair is arranged differently on film and in studio.

The Monster of Peladon

The miner played by Max Faulkner is killed twice, once by the Ice Warriors and once by Eckersley, yet is still alive in a later scene in the throne room.

Genesis of the Daleks

The Doctor's brown overcoat vanishes, and then turns up again at the end. He has it on when he and Sarah and Harry start using the Time Ring, but not when they are pictured spinning through space, and it's not in **Revenge of the Cybermen**. The same goes for his hat. But at the start of **Terror of the Zygons**, coat and hat are both back, although not necessarily worn by the Doctor.

The Robots of Death

When V6 has its hand trapped in Toos' door, it's only the hand on the robot's side, but it's the whole sleeve on hers.

The Talons of Weng-Chiang

In part six, the Doctor throws an axe which embeds itself between the eyes of the dragon in Greel's lair, and then Leela blasts the same area with her revolver. However, at the end of the scene when the Doctor takes everyone off for muffins, there is no sign of the axe or bullet damage on the dragon.

The Invasion of Time

At the beginning, the Doctor's scarf is on the TARDIS hatstand. The Doctor is outside with the Vardans – and wearing his scarf.

The Stones of Blood

The OB sequences set at night are in day-for-night, i.e. fairly light really. Unfortunately, various exterior sequences recorded in studio and interspersed with the film work look like the sky is pitch-black.

The Horns of Nimon

In between his death scene and the shot of the nuclear furnace about to explode, Soldeed's body disappears. (The TARDIS seems to have vanished from outside the Power Complex in the same sequence, although one could argue that the Doctor and Romana have just left in it.)

Meglos

Two Gaztak warriors are killed in the raid on Tigella, but they can be seen among the extras when the Gaztaks return to Zolpha-Thura.

Full Circle

The Outlers sneak into the TARDIS and creep up on Romana. Despite the fact they have just come in from the swampy ground outside where they have lived rough for an unspecified period, we are treated to a close-up of their extremely clean new shoes.

Logopolis

The inconsistencies in the use of the controls on the TARDIS console are legion, but one notable example is the big red lever, used since Peter Davison's stories as the door control. In the eighteenth season, when it first appears, it is not the door control, and it isn't even always on the side of the console facing the doors. Three different controls are used to open the door through the course of the story.

Castrovalva

*In **Logopolis** and the pre-title sequence for **Castrovalva**, the Fourth Doctor is wearing boots. Yet despite keeping the rest of the clothing when he changes, the Fifth Doctor is miraculously wearing shoes. The only other instance of clothing-regeneration is when the First Doctor changes into the Second, complete with a whole new outfit (apart from his ring, which falls off later).*

Earthshock

In part four, Scott and three troopers return to the TARDIS, but the last of them, a woman, is grabbed by a Cyberman. Inside the TARDIS, the woman and one of the male troopers come in, and with Scott, dispose of the Cyberman. Scott and the troopers leave, and when we see them again, there are just two male troopers.

Frontios

The bar Tegan puts across the door moves from the middle of the handles to the top. Lucky that, as it allows her to escape.

The Happiness Patrol and Silver Nemesis

*Ace is wearing Flowerchild's earring on her jacket, despite the fact that she doesn't acquire it until the subsequent story, **The Greatest Show in the Galaxy**.*

RELATIVE DIMENSIONS

Not to imply that there is anything iffy going on, of course, but there are a number of occasions where people who just happen to be related to each other by blood or marriage just happen to work on the same **Doctor Who** story. We haven't widened the scope of this to cover such people who have *ever* worked on the show, which would include Ann Davies and her husband Richard Briers in **The Dalek Invasion of Earth** and **Paradise Towers** respectively. However, there are a few temptingly close calls, such as Mark Strickson's wife, Julie Brennon, who also appeared in **Paradise Towers**, only three years after her husband left the show.

- *Production Unit Manager Angela Smith's daughter, Alys Dyer, appeared as Baby Pangol in* **The Leisure Hive**, *and along with her sister, Lucy, as children in* **The Trial of a Time Lord** *(parts one to four).*

- *Production Secretary Sarah Lee's mother, Lynda Baron, appeared as Captain Wrack in* **Enlightenment**.

- *Director Rex Tucker's daughter, Jane, was an extra in* **The Gunfighters**.

- *Patrick Troughton's son, David, was a non-speaking guard in* **The Enemy of the World** *and Private Moor in* **The War Games**.

- *Producer Peter Bryant's wife, Shirley Cooklin, was cast as Kaftan in the first story he oversaw,* **The Tomb of the Cybermen**.

- *Producer Derrick Sherwin's wife, Jane, played Lady Jennifer Buckingham in* **The War Games**.

- *Fraser Hines' cousin, Ian Hines, was a Central European guard in* **The Enemy of the World** *and a toy soldier in* **The Mind Robber**. *Hamish Wilson, who took over from Fraser to play Jamie for some of* **The Mind Robber**, *is another cousin.*

- *Deborah Watling's father, Jack, appeared as Professor Travers in* **The Abominable Snowmen** *and* **The Web of Fear**.

- *Director's Assistant on* **The Ark**, *Thelma Helsby, was working with her sister, Eileen, who played Venussa in episodes 3 and 4.*

- *Make-up Supervisor, Sonia Markham, was applying cosmetics to, among others, her sister, Petra, in* **The Crusade**.

- *Writer Don Houghton's wife, Pik-Sen Lim, featured as Captain Chin-Lee, as well as* *coaching Jon Pertwee in Hokkien, in **The Mind of Evil**.*

🎬 *William Marlowe and his wife, Fernanda, both appeared in **The Mind of Evil**. The latter got a bonus by being hired for the following story, where her character, Corporal Bell, explained that there were freak weather conditions where Axos had landed (a line inserted to explain the ludicrous extremes of weather found by the hapless production team on location).*

🎬 *Director Michael Briant's wife, Monique, was an extra on his first story, **Colony in Space** (but she also appeared in other stories, such as **The Seeds of Death**, which had nothing to do with him).*

🎬 *Director Douglas Camfield cast his wife, Sheila Dunn, in **The Daleks' Master Plan** (as Blossom le Favre in the episode **The Feast of Steven)**, **The Invasion** (as the computer voice and 'phone girl'), and in **Inferno** (as Petra Williams).*

🎬 *Director Lennie Mayne's wife, Frances Pidgeon, appeared for him in **The Monster of Peladon** as Thalira's (non-speaking) attendant, and **The Hand of Fear** as Miss Jackson.*

🎬 *A triple-whammy: Caroline John's husband, Geoffrey Beevers, appeared in **The Ambassadors of Death** as UNIT's Private Johnson. The story's production assistant (floor manager) was her brother, Nick John.*

🎬 *Sylvester McCoy's sons, Joe and Sam Kent-Smith, appeared as small Haemovores in **The Curse of Fenric**.*

🎬 *Not the same sort of relationship as the others here, but producer John Nathan-Turner's dog Pepsi made several appearances, including **K-9 and Company: A Girl's Best Friend**, and **The Curse of Fenric**.*

🎬 *Not legally recognised, but a relationship still – Katy Manning's boyfriend, Stewart Bevan, co-starred in **The Green Death**, and got the girl…*

🎬 *Again a slight twist of the rules, but for good solid romantic reasons: Michael Craze and production assistant, Edwina Verner, met and later married after, during the pre-filming at Ealing studios for **The Tenth Planet**, she threw a polystyrene 'snowball' at his still-healing broken nose...*

🎬 *Hero Trew, daughter of Ken the costume designer, appeared as one of the schoolchildren in **Remembrance of the Daleks***

HERE WE GO AGAIN...

That is, bits, rather than whole stories of **Doctor Who** which get a second airing. These fall into two categories, actual flashbacks, and bits of film or tape used twice, where it was hoped we wouldn't notice. Note that we haven't included instances in early stories where the recap of the previous episode was in the form of a filmed telerecording of the cliffhanger – in the days before easy videotape editing, it was necessary either to do that or re-enact the last scene. Here are just some of the more notable examples.

Reused footage

The Dalek Invasion of Earth
A close-up of a Dalek gun firing is used more than once.

Revenge of the Cybermen and **The Android Invasion**
Both use the same footage of a US Apollo rocket taking off, as seen from the gantry.

The War Games
*Footage of explosions in No-Man's Land is used more than once, and the scene of Romans charging in episode seven is the same as that used in episode two. In episode ten, when the Doctor is fleeing from the Time Lords, the TARDIS lands on the sea – in fact a clip taken from **Fury from the Deep** – then in space – a clip from **The Web of Fear**. Later, when Zoe is returned to where she came from, footage of the 'Wheel' space station from **The Wheel in Space** is used as an establishing shot.*

Underworld
Plagued with production problems due to its weighty use of CSO, it resorted to reusing sequences of guards running down cave tunnels.

The Power of Kroll
During the sequence of the Doctor, Romana and Rohm-Dutt being chased by Swampies, a shot of several Swampies in pursuit is used twice, although it is edited slightly differently.

The Green Death
Footage of explosions and of the helicopter bombing maggots is used more than once.

The Leisure Hive
A shot of an Argolin walking along a corridor is used twice in different episodes.

The Ark In Space
Another triple-whammy: In the sequence in where Rogin and Harry fire at the Wirrn grub, a cutaway to Sarah's horrified reaction is used twice. Despite the fact they are now in a different room, the same shot is used again in part four to show her reaction to the Doctor electrocuting a Wirrn.

The Invasion

*Stretching a point here, but the stock footage of radars twirling round is used almost to exhaustion in this story. Almost, as it has recovered sufficiently to reappear (in colour, this time) in **Spearhead from Space**.*

The Armageddon Factor and **Meglos**

Both these stories feature time-loops, treating us to the same footage again and again...

The Wheel in Space and **The Trial of a Time Lord**

These two stories in particular are notable for their repeated use of the same establishing shots...of a space station in both cases.

Flashbacks

The Celestial Toymaker

*Scenes from Steven and Dodo's past are shown by the Toymaker as a demonstration of his power. Dodo is seen at her mother's funeral (specially shot footage), while Steven sees himself in clips from **The Daleks' Master Plan** and **The Massacre of St. Bartholomew's Eve**.*

The Ark

When the TARDIS returns in episode 3, the Monoids view scenes from episode 2 of the ship leaving.

The Wheel in Space

*At the end, the Doctor shows what Zoe is letting herself in for if she joins him by 'mentally' projecting a scene from **The Evil of the Daleks** on the TARDIS scanner. This was in fact to trail a repeat of the story during the summer break in the series.*

Frontier in Space

When the Doctor is being mind-probed, the screen shows footage from episode one of the TARDIS and the Ogrons entering the spaceship.

Planet of the Spiders

*Features an excerpt from **Carnival of Monsters** when Professor Clegg holds the sonic screwdriver while in the Doctor's IRIS machine. Later, Tommy's memories of what has been happening to him are indicated as flashbacks of those events, as is the Doctor's memory of visiting the cave of the Great One.*

Logopolis

*The regeneration sequence features clips from Tom Baker stories of villains and companions (except the Brigadier, represented by a clip from **Invasion of the Dinosaurs**).*

Earthshock

> *The Cybermen review images of past incarnations of the Doctor, with clips from* **The Tenth Planet, The Wheel in Space** *(standing in for* **The Tomb of the Cybermen**, *which was not known to exist at the time) and* **Revenge of the Cybermen**.

Mawdryn Undead

> *The Brigadier's returning memories are shown as clips from* **The Three Doctors, The Web of Fear** *(a scene from episode 1, as the episodes with Lethbridge-Stewart in do not exist),* **The Invasion, The Claws of Axos, Day of the Daleks, Robot** *and* **Terror of the Zygons**.

The Five Doctors

> *Opens with a scene from the end of* **The Dalek Invasion of Earth**, *where the Doctor promises to come back to see Susan at some time in the future.*

Resurrection of the Daleks

> *The Doctor is forced to recall clips of his old selves and companions (curiously omitting Leela), represented by clips from stories. The exception is Katarina, who is represented by a photograph.*

YOU'RE SERIOUS, AREN'T YOU?

IN-JOKES

Knowing references and in-jokes of one sort or another occasionally crop up in the programme. Sometimes they can seem totally obscure, but a close scrutiny of the programme's credits can help to bring enlightenment. Here's a sample of some of the more accessible examples.

The Daleks' Master Plan

*The Christmas episode, **The Feast of Steven**, features a character called Man in Mackintosh, who accosts the Doctor in the police station. The Doctor says he knows him from Jaffa. The character was played by Reg Pritchard, who played market trader Ben Daheer in **The Crusade**.*

The Web of Fear

Colonel Lethbridge-Stewart's predecessor had been Colonel Pemberton – a nod to the former story editor, Victor Pemberton, who worked with writers Mervyn Haisman and Henry Lincoln on the first Yeti story.

Doctor Who and the Silurians

Has a Private Upton. This may be a coincidence, but Sue Upton was the director's assistant.

The Ambassadors of Death

Features a van with James Bond-style changeable name signs on the sides. The firms advertised were 'Hayhoe Launderers Co.' and 'Silcock Bakeries' – named after the story's assistant floor manager Margot Hayhoe and director's assistant, Pauline Silcock.

Colony in Space

*The Doctor remarks to Jo that the last person the Brigadier's agents arrested on suspicion of being the Master turned out to be the Spanish ambassador – a reference to the fact that Roger Delgado once played the Spanish ambassador in a 1950s swashbuckling series, in which he had a swordfight with one Barry Letts, then an actor, by 1971 producer of **Doctor Who.***

Robot

Tom Baker's Doctor, newly regenerated, remarks on looking into a mirror that his nose is a definite improvement – a reference to Jon Pertwee's sensitivity about unflattering camera angles of his own proboscis.

The Ark in Space

One of the technological devices the Doctor dates the space station by is a 'Bennett oscillator' — Rodney Bennett was the director.

The Robots of Death

Grimwade's syndrome — the technical name for robophobia, was named after the show's production assistant (floor manager) Peter Grimwade, later a writer and director on **Doctor Who**.

The Pirate Planet

A set of galactic co-ordinates was actually a BBC internal phone number.

Logopolis

The Master apparently beams a signal from the Pharos Project to co-ordinates that just happened to match part of Anthony Ainley's own phone number at the time.

The Armageddon Factor

Discerning viewers might well surmise that Valentine Dyall was unlikely to be the White Guardian, as he was famous in former years for playing radio's macabre story-teller, The Man in Black.

Shada

Only revealed widely on the release of the video, the cancelled serial features a number of contrived Douglas Adams jokes, one being Professor Chronotis trying to remember Chris Parsons' name by going through the alphabet. He gets stuck on 'B', repeats it, and the Doctor and Romana chorus the next letter.

Meglos

Around the time that Tom Baker announced he was relinquishing the lead role, Lieutenant Brotadac has the line, said of Baker as Meglos, 'Do you think he'll let me have that [coat] — now that he's finished playing the Doctor?'

Dragonfire

Sabalom Glitz has a line, accompanied by knowing glances between him and Sylvester, about the treasure map being 'the real McCoy'. The story's character names are also in-references to figures in film history and theory, even down to Ace's real name, Dorothy, referring to **The Wizard of Oz**. *The Doctor's philosophical discussion with the guard, Arnheim, where the latter floors him with the query, 'What do you think of the assertion that the semiotic thickness of a performed text varies according to the redundancy of auxiliary performance codes?' features the kind of media-studies-babble familiar to bemused readers of the academic work* **Doctor Who: The Unfolding Text**.

Timelash

The android's sing-song voice is used to comic effect when it says 'Yes indeed she was,' in the same tones as the communication music in **Close Encounters of the Third Kind**. *In the same story, the Doctor says to Herbert: 'To be perfectly frank, Herbert,' a play on the name of another famous sf writer (of whom Colin Baker is a fan).*

Remembrance of the Daleks

The nickname of Group Captain Gilmore, 'Chunky', was a cast in-joke from rehearsals.

The Greatest Show in the Galaxy

*Is one long in-joke, in that on one level, it is a satire on **Doctor Who** itself. Especially cutting is the character of Whizzkid, apparently a dig at the kind of sad fan who is totally obssessed with his pet subject to the exclusion of all else. Of course, we don't know anyone like that, less still are we like that ourselves. Honest.*

Doctor Who: The Movie

Features a character called Professor Wagg, named after the original co-producer Peter Wagg.

DALEKS CUTAWAY

Most Dalek stories have attempted to show more Daleks than the three or four affordable manned examples. Most Dalek stories have also shown Daleks being destroyed messily. Both these circumstances demand the use of subterfuges – empty dummy Daleks, model Daleks, or, infamously in the 1960s, photo blow-up Daleks. We have not included the empty Dalek in **The Space Museum** (where the Doctor hides) in this list, as it's an exhibit and supposed to be empty.

The Daleks

Dummy Dalek with collapsible middle section used for the one Ian had formerly occupied which is zapped by the other Daleks. There is a 'crowd scene' of Daleks in a later episode using photo blow-ups.

The Dalek Invasion of Earth

Dummy Daleks include those rammed by Barbara and Jenny's dustcart, and the ones manhandled by the revolting prisoners in episode 6. Model shots of the bomb which is to be dropped into the Earth's core include a working miniature Dalek.

The Chase

A model Dalek rises from the sand at the end of episode 1. What must surely be a dummy topples into Ian's trap in episode 2. There is a photo blow-up Dalek in their ship's lift in episode 3, and either side of it are a pair of Daleks from the cinema film, empty and minus their bases. A dummy Dalek is shown toppling into the sea from the Mary Celeste and another is hurled about by Frankenstein's Monster. A film Dalek turns up in episode 5 in the Mechanus jungle, motionless. Dummy ones explode and collapse in the filmed fight sequence with the Mechanoids.

The Daleks' Master Plan

Collapsible sections and dummy Daleks are used at the end of episode 12, when the Time Destructor destroys them.

The Power of the Daleks

The production line of new Daleks is represented using models; the massed Dalek army involves photo blow-ups (one of which sways in the breeze caused by a real Dalek going past it). The Daleks blowing up at the end are dummies and models.

The Evil of the Daleks

*There are two Daleks featured at the end of episode 2, but only one is occupied (to avoid paying another actor for such a short sequence). The climactic Dalek-on-Dalek fight scenes are achieved with dummies and models (as with **Power**, these are often commercial Dalek toys).*

The Mind of Evil

As with the other old monsters featured, the Dalek is a BBC publicity still cut-out.

Planet of the Daleks

The Dalek at the end of episode one is empty. Dummy Daleks are used for 'crowd' scenes. Models are employed for the scene of one on a hover-disc being clouted with a rock, and for the Dalek army that gets gunged.

Death to the Daleks

Dummies are used for Daleks required to explode, and there are scenes at the start of part two involving four Daleks at once, one of which is obviously unoccupied (there were only three operators).

Genesis of the Daleks

There are few scenes involving more than three Daleks, but some shots late in the story involve unoccupied dummies.

Destiny of the Daleks

Several dummy Daleks were built to be blown up in episode four. In some of the sequences of the Daleks advancing across the desert landscape of Skaro, they are all-too-obviously the dummy Daleks being 'walked' along from behind. Watch also for the sequence when Davros sends the Daleks on their suicide mission, while a dummy Dalek is wobbled around behind him for effect.

The Five Doctors

The sole featured Dalek had a stunt double to blow up for it.

Resurrection of the Daleks

Polystyrene dummies are used to fall out of the first floors of buildings, get blown up and thrash about greenly.

Revelation of the Daleks

The dummies have similar tasks here, getting blown up a lot – especially by Orcini's bastic-headed bullets. A Sevans large model Dalek kit was also used for the one that materialises in the cellars.

Remembrance of the Daleks

An empty Dalek was used to go upstairs for the part one cliffhanger. Numerous stunt double Daleks get blown up, including those comprehensively zapped by the Special Weapons Dalek.

OF COURSE, HE WILL LOOK QUITE DIFFERENT
IN-STORY CAST CHANGES

It may seem peculiar to have the same character played by more than one person in a story, but there are many occasions in **Doctor Who** where the actor's identity is concealed, so it doesn't matter too much. There are, however, one or two other situations… (but note that we are not talking about stunt doubles for actors.) We do include some notable occasions where rewriting is necessary, and although a character as well as an actor has changed, it's essentially the same role.

The Three, Five and Two Doctors

*The Doctor, of course. These are not really cast changes as such, but regenerations are. In fact, there are only two regenerations where the Doctor is played by two actors in the same story in the sense that both have lines to speak. These are: Davison-Baker (**The Caves of Androzani**) and McCoy-McGann (**Dr Who – The Movie**). However, Patrick Troughton, Tom Baker and Peter Davison all appeared in their predecessor's final episode.*

The Daleks

Although not a character in the strict sense, Michael Summerton stops being a Dalek operator after three episodes and is replaced by Peter Murphy.

The Macra Terror

Chicki is played by Sandra Bryant in episode 1 and Karol Keyes in episode 4. It is possible this was due to illness – it might well not have been possible to rewrite the part for another character as at this point episodes were being recorded on the Saturday before transmission.

The Crusade

The character of Ibrahim was played by Tutte Lemkow. However, his scene in episode 3 was with William Russell as Ian, who was allocated a holiday that week and pre-filmed his performance. As Lemkow was not available for the filming, his part was rewritten for 'Turkish bandit' who was revealed to be Ibrahim's brother (played by David Brewster).

The Romans

The Centurion (Dennis Edwards) was a speaking part in episode 1, but only a corpse in episode 2, so extra Vez Delahunt was hired to perform that role (not so much a walk-on as a lie-down-and-don't-move).

The Dominators

Similarly, as Balan is killed at the end of episode 4, extra John Tucker replaced him for episode 5.

The Brain of Morbius

In parts one and two, the 'headless monster body' is required merely to lie on a bed and twitch, so extra Alan Crisp played the part, rather than waste Stuart Fell's time.

The Mind Robber

Yet another quick mention for Hamish Wilson who played Jamie for an episode-and-a-bit due to chicken pox setting its sights on Fraser Hines.

The Green Death

Illness forced Tony Adams to bow out as Elgin after two of three recording sessions. A quick rewrite later, and the character of Mr James appeared from nowhere to fill the gaping hole in the story, played by stalwart, Roy Skelton.

Day of the Daleks

Jean McFarlane who played Styles' secretary, Miss Paget, was unavailable for a scene in the final episode where Styles is persuaded to evacuate Auderley House. Her line was instead given to Styles' new aide played by Desmond Verini.

Terror of the Autons

Norman Stanley is the Master – the only time when one of the Master's disguises has involved employing another actor.

Invasion of the Dinosaurs

It seems likely that the character of Private Ogden was originally in parts five and six as well as parts one and two. The main reason for this supposition is that Ogden is played by George Bryson, and his replacement, played by Colin Bell, is one Private Bryson.

THE LONG AND THE SHORT OF IT

Traditionally, classically, mostly, or whatever, **Doctor Who** is associated with twenty-five minute episodes, or rather slots, with the recommended duration being twenty-four minutes thirty seconds. The shortest billed time for episodes were for all episodes of **The Mind Robber** and part four of **Meglos**, at twenty minutes each; the longest billed time, discounting compilation repeats, was for **The Five Doctors** at 90 minutes, followed closely by **Doctor Who: The Movie** at 85 minutes. Other oddities of billed duration are **Resurrection of the Daleks**, with part one advertised as 45 minutes, and part two as fifty, then the 22nd season in 1985 all billed as 45 minutes. Various 'normal' episodes have been billed as running 30 minutes (episode 4 of **The Invisible Enemy**, for example), but the last episode of **The Trial of a Time Lord** genuinely had a half-hour slot to fill.

The longest and shortest actual durations in the various slots are as follows:

- Longest 20' – 22'27" (**The Mind Robber** episode 1)

- Shortest 20' – 18'00" (**The Mind Robber** episode 5)

  *Since **The Mind Robber** was the only complete story billed as 20' per episode, this doesn't leave much room for manoeuvre. The last episode of **Meglos** was also billed as 20' and ran to 19'30" – making it the fourth shortest (by a second).*

- Longest 25' – 26'57" (**Marco Polo** episode 2)

  *Oddly there are numerous episodes over 25', and a total of 10 over 26' (mostly in the sixties, although the most recent was **Destiny of the Daleks** episode four in 1979).*

- Shortest 25' – 20'29" (**Fury from the Deep** episode 3)

  *Despite the fact that it is billed in a 20' slot, **The Mind Robber** episode 1 is actually longer than 31 episodes which are billed as 25'. Of these, three (counting this one) are under 21'. The others are **Image of the Fendahl** part four (20'32") and **The Leisure Hive** part two (20'43").*

- Only 30' – (**The Trial of a Time Lord** part fourteen)

  It actually ran to 29'30"

- Longest 45' – 46'24" (**Resurrection of the Daleks** part one)

- Shortest 45' – 43'51" (**The Two Doctors** part two)

- Only 50' – 46'52" (**Resurrection of the Daleks** part two)

  *The only other possible entry in this category is **K-9 and Company: A Girl's Best Friend**, the duration of which was 49'56")*

⬛ Only 85' – 84'32" in UK (**Doctor Who: The Movie**)

⬛ Only 90' – 90'20" (**The Five Doctors**)

Other timing oddities

There are eight episodes which exactly fit the 25' slot:

The Ark *episode 2,* **The Underwater Menace** *episode 2,* **The War Games** *episode 1,* **Doctor Who and the Silurians** *episode 4,* **Robot** *part two,* **The Hand of Fear** *part four,* **The Horns of Nimon** *part two and* **The Caves of Androzani** *part two.*

⬛ There are just seventeen episodes which are exactly the BBC recommended length of 24'30":

The Daleks *episode 4,* **The Daleks' Master Plan** *episode 3,* **The Ark** *episode 1,* **The Highlanders** *episode 1,* **The Evil of the Daleks** *episode 3,* **The Invasion** *episode one,* **The Sea Devils** *episode two,* **Genesis of the Daleks** *part one,* **The Android Invasion** *parts two and four,* **The Deadly Assassin** *part four,* **The Talons of Weng-Chiang** *part four,* **Time-Flight** *part four,* **Mawdryn Undead** *part three,* **Paradise Towers** *part three,* **Remembrance of the Daleks** *part three and* **The Greatest Show in the Galaxy** *part three.*

⬛ Compilations:

These are difficult beasts, as they can be compiled from different length stories, and some adventures can stand more being chopped out of them than others. Compilations such as **The Sontaran Experiment** *and* **The Robots of Death** *(repeated in two parts on the last day of 1977 and the first of 1978) are basically uncut, as was the last compilation screened (***The Awakening***, in 1984).* **Genesis of the Daleks** *suffered twice being hacked about, to an 85'53" version in 1975 and for two 45' slots in 1982 as part of the* **Doctor Who and the Monsters** *repeat series. The longest 'cut' compilation was* **Planet of the Spiders** *at 105'14", from a six-part original; the 'shortest' (most cut, proportionately) was* **Day of the Daleks** *at 59'46" out of four episodes. There is also the phenomenon of, for want of a better word, de-compilations; in the UK there were repeat versions of* **The Five Doctors** *and* **Revelation of the Daleks** *in a four-part episodic format.*

⬛ Shortened repeat episodes:

The Deadly Assassin *is almost unique in that less than three seconds was cut from the end of part three when it was repeated – following complaints about the freeze-frame of the Doctor's head held underwater. The sequence and freeze-frame were restored to the BBC Video release (strangely, from a VHS copy rather than* *from the reprise in part four).*

Also unique is the repeat of **Carnival of Monsters** *in the Five Faces of Doctor Who season on BBC2 which had a sequence at the end of part 4 shortened to remove the sight of Pletrac's headpiece coming adrift from his real head.*

The Time Meddler *was slightly abridged on its repeat as the BBC no longer hold a complete copy. Episode one was pretty much intact due to the generosity of a 'private collector' who loaned his/her own copy.*

MY APOTHEOSIS
STUNTMEN AND EXTRAS GIVEN THEIR BIG CHANCE

There are occasions when, during rehearsals or recording, a part which is written for a supporting artist suddenly seems to require a little bit more. Thus, walk-ons or extras can sometimes be promoted to 'walk-on 2' (which means they can deliver a line germane to their character's profession, such as a bus conductor saying 'Any more fares please'). However, sometimes slightly more involved lines can make a difference to the plot development, and the role becomes a 'speaking' part with a credit. Some of these performers later get even bigger roles by virtue of their vast acting experience (as opposed to talent).

- Pat Gorman
  > One of the most widely used walk-ons in the series for many years, he has been upgraded to small speaking parts many times. His most involved roles are that of the UNIT corporal in part two of **Invasion of the Dinosaurs** and the Thal soldier in part two of **Genesis of the Daleks**, looking for slave labour for the Thal rocket.

- John Cannon
  > Again a much-used supporting artist, he is notable as power station worker Elgin in **The Hand of Fear** and as the less-than-enthusiastic guard escorting Princess Astra to her doom in **The Armageddon Factor**.

- Royston Farrell
  > In **The Claws of Axos**, extra Farrell – everyone else in charge of the Nuton power complex having met with a grisly death – has to warn of the consequences if the particle accelerator goes out of control – his big line: 'Bang!'

- Steve Brunswick
  > Cast as an extra in **The Time Warrior**, he was given a small speaking part as the guard on the gate of Irongron's castle when the Doctor and Sarah arrive disguised as friars. He gives an interesting performance.

- Terry Walsh
  > Omnipresent stuntman in the 70s, he gets several small roles including the guard captain in **The Monster of Peladon**, Mensch the tame(-ish) Swampie in **The Power of Kroll** and Doran the engineer in **The Creature from the Pit**, who is hurled down the latter and squashed by the former.

- Alan Chuntz
  > Stuntman, menacing chauffeur in **The Seeds of Doom**, soundly thumped by the Doctor at his most **Sweeney**-esque.

Derek Ware

Stuntman and fight arranger, appears as the bus conductor who thinks that Ian and Barbara have been to the moon when they ask for two 'threes' in **The Chase**. *He was also Private Wyatt in* **Inferno**, *turning into a Primord. It is interesting to note that he did not perform the filmed stunt of his own death, in case he was injured, as he was required for studio recording. His stunt double was Roy Scammel, who, strangely, also played the soldier who shoots him.*

Max Faulkner

Again a stuntman who graduated to parts which did not require stunt work, or that was not their primary function. His major roles are as Corporal Adams in **The Android Invasion** *and Nesbin in* **The Invasion of Time**.

John Levene

Undoubtedly the most outstanding example, someone raised from the ranks of the 'chorus' to be a lead character in the programme. Levene worked as an extra in **The Moonbase**, *then director Douglas Camfield, who had worked with him on* **Z Cars**, *cast him as a Yeti in* **The Web of Fear**. *This led to his role as Corporal, later Sergeant, later still RSM, Benton.*

A HOLIDAY FOR THE DOCTOR
EPISODES WHERE A REGULAR DOESN'T APPEAR

This list is concerned mainly with the 1960s, when episodes were recorded individually, and in very long stretches. This meant that regular artists were guaranteed a certain number of weeks off in a season, which were covered for either by writing them out, or pre-filming short sequences in advance. Any later instances are for different reasons. We have not included examples of *semi-regulars* who were often absent for narrative reasons (the best examples being the main UNIT personnel).

William Hartnell – **The Keys of Marinus** episodes 3 and 4
  The Doctor disappears for two weeks, purportedly hurrying on to Millenius. (Note that Hartnell's contract specified that he be credited no matter what, hence his presence in the end roller captions and Radio Times *listings for episodes he missed.)*

Carole Ann Ford – **The Aztecs** episodes 2 and 3
  Susan appears briefly on film only.

Jacqueline Hill – **The Sensorites** episodes 4 and 5
  Barbara stays on the spaceship when everyone else goes down to the Sense Sphere, following only in episode 6.

William Russell – **The Reign of Terror** episodes 2 and 3
  Ian is locked in a cell for two weeks, appearing only on film. He does feature in the trial scene with Susan and Barbara, but is careful to stand well apart from them – as they are not *on film.*

William Hartnell – **The Dalek Invasion of Earth** episode 4
  An unscheduled absence, as Hartnell was involved in an accident on set. Although not badly hurt, he had a week's leave, and was doubled for by Edmund Warwick (although the Doctor loses consciousness almost at once).

Jacqueline Hill – **The Web Planet** episode 3
  A week off as Barbara is imprisoned in the Crater of Needles, unseen.

William Russell – **The Crusade** episode 3
  Ian goes off through the desert in search of Barbara and is waylaid by bandits... on film.

William Hartnell – **The Space Museum** episode 3
  Frozen by the Moroks (ouch!) as preparation for being put into the eponymous archive, Hartnell only appears as a telerecorded recap from episode 2.

William Hartnell – **The Time Meddler** episode 2

Imprisoned by the Monk, the Doctor makes his presence felt only as a telerecorded insert of the end of episode 1, and an unseen but briefly vocal presence throwing his breakfast back at his captor.

William Hartnell, Peter Purves and Maureen O'Brien – **Dalek Cutaway**
The regulars being contractually unobliged to appear in this extra episode tacked onto the programme's second recording block, the stars of the show were for one week the Daleks, plus Edward de Souza as space agent Marc Cory. Confusingly, (but contractually), Hartnell was still credited.

William Hartnell – **The Massacre of St. Bartholomew's Eve** episode 2
Hartnell appears briefly in this episode on film and as the Abbot of Amboise, not the Doctor (although we are led to believe they are one and the same). Hartnell is in episode 3, but again the Doctor isn't.

William Hartnell – **The Celestial Toymaker**
The Doctor is made invisible and voiceless, and so appears only as a silent hand in episode 3, playing the Trilogic Game (and it's not Hartnell's hand, but extra, Albert Ward's). Hartnell's appearance in episode 2 is on film also.

William Hartnell – **The Savages** episode 3
An honorary, but not actual, absence. Having had his life essence drained and put into Jano, the Doctor has no lines and precious little to do in this episode, being guided around by Steven and Dodo for the most part. Frederick Jaeger gets to do his Hartnell impression instead.

William Hartnell – **The Tenth Planet**
As mentioned elsewhere, Hartnell was brought back specially after his regular contract had expired to do one last story, and was unwell. Doubled for in the film sequences, he was also absent for the third episode in the electronic studio.

Anneke Wills – **The Power of the Daleks** episode 4
Polly is kidnapped by the rebels on Vulcan, and gets a week off as a result.

Michael Craze – **The Power of the Daleks** episode 5
Not to be outdone, Ben suffers a similar fate while trying to free Polly.

Michael Craze and Anneke Wills – **The Faceless Ones** episodes 3 to 5
With seeming indecent haste to be rid of them, the characters of Ben and Polly disappear in episode 2 and only turn up again at the end of episode 6, to say goodbye.

Patrick Troughton – **The Evil of the Daleks** episode 4
The Doctor appears only in film sequences, as he monitors Jamie's attempts to rescue Victoria.

🛈 Fraser Hines and Deborah Watling – **The Enemy of the World** episode 4
Their cover blown in their attempts to infiltrate Salamander's headquarters, Jamie and Victoria are locked up for an episode.

🛈 Patrick Troughton – **The Wheel in Space** episode 2
Knocked unconscious, the Doctor lies comatose (in the person of Chris Jeffries) while the Silver Carrier, and the TARDIS aboard it, is endangered.

🛈 Fraser Hines – **The Mind Robber** episode 2
As detailed elsewhere, several times, Hines was ill and had to be replaced surreally by Hamish Wilson. His only contribution to the episode was a videotaped insert made later and edited in.

🛈 Wendy Padbury – **The Invasion** episode three
Zoe and Isobel are captured by Packer's men and sent to IE's factory in the countryside.

🛈 Fraser Hines – **The Invasion** episode eight
Jamie is shot slightly in episode seven, and can only appear on film in episode eight (on Doctor's orders?).

🛈 Patrick Troughton – **The Seeds of Death** episode four
Gassed by a seed pod and rescued just in time from transmat into space, the Doctor lies unconscious again, doubled for by Tommy Laird.

🛈 Patrick Troughton, Fraser Hines and Wendy Padbury – **The Space Pirates** episode six
*All scenes with the regulars were shot on film in advance, so they would be free for the extensive location work required on **The War Games**. This was the second time in the show's history (after **Dalek Cutaway**) when none of the main cast were present for a recording session.*

🛈 Caroline John – **Inferno** episode 5
Only absent in a sense, as she still played her alternative universe self, but 'our' Liz Shaw did not appear in episode 5.

🛈 Sarah Sutton – **Kinda** parts two and three
*Sutton was contracted for only twenty-four out of twenty-six episodes in the series, possibly as this story was originally written for a smaller cast of regulars and did not lend itself to adaptation. Nyssa is seen collapsing at the end of the previous story, **Four to Doomsday**, and the Doctor leaves her asleep in the TARDIS for a couple of episodes.*

🛈 Colin Baker and Nicola Bryant – **Revelation of the Daleks** part one
Not quite the same thing for sure by this time, but in terms of broadcast, the two leads only appear on film in this episode.

65

WE WILL SURVIVE...

Fans lament the sorry state of the BBC's holdings of **Doctor Who**, although it's a lot better than for some other programmes. At the time of writing, 110 episodes do not exist in complete or near-complete form – some episodes have minor cuts made by overseas broadcasters, others made in colour only exist in black and white. Of the episodes not held in complete form there are a few from which short clips do exist:

Galaxy 4
> *A clip from episode 1 exists in the BBC* Lively Arts *documentary* **Whose Doctor Who**, *originally transmitted on 3rd April 1977.*

The Daleks' Master Plan
> *Original film sequences from episodes 1 and 2 (with sound for those from 2) exist. Short sequences from episodes 3 and 4 exist in* **Blue Peter** *editions shown 25/10/71 and 5/11/73 respectively.*

The War Machines
> *The BBC's copy is slightly cut, but excised material held by the Australian censors department has now been reinserted (for video release) making the story almost complete. 59' is still missing from part 3, and a single short scene from part 4.*

The Smugglers
> *Cuts made by Australian censors exist, as does a home movie made during location filming showing some of the action being shot.*

The Tenth Planet
> *The regeneration sequence from the end of otherwise-missing episode 4 exists on the recording of* **Blue Peter** *from 5/11/73.*

The Power of the Daleks
> *Excerpts from the story exist, one as part of an Australian documentary programme, another as a clip shown on* **Blue Peter** *on 27th November 1967.*

The Highlanders
> *Cuts made by Australian censors exist, also a short out-take sequence of production assistant (floor manager) Fiona Cumming with clapperboard.*

The Underwater Menace
> *Australian censors' cuts from episodes 1 and 2 exist.*

The Macra Terror
> *Cuts by Australian censors exist, from episodes 2 and 3.*

The Abominable Snowmen
> *A short sequence from episode 4 exists of a Yeti by the TARDIS, as well as a home movie made during location filming.*

Fury from the Deep

> *The TARDIS landing sequence survives as part of* **The War Games** *episode ten, in which it was reused. Australian censors' cuts also exist from other episodes.*

The Wheel in Space

> *A short sequence cut by Australian censors from episode 4 exists.*

Terror of the Autons

> *Although the BBC hold a restored colour version, made from a 525 line off-air colour recording and a black and white film recording, part of the opening laboratory sequence exists in its original 625 line colour format, a dub made for the* **Nationwide** *interview with Katy Manning when she left the programme.*

NOT AGAIN!

ACTORS USED FREQUENTLY BY THE SAME DIRECTOR

Certain directors have informal 'repertory companies' of actors they frequently use in medium-sized and small roles. This list is, of course, confined to **Doctor Who** appearances, and to those actors who have been cast at least three times by the same director. Douglas Camfield is perhaps the prime exponent of this phenomenon, and there are several others actors making only two appearances for him. In addition, he was responsible for the casting of Nicholas Courtney and John Levene in the UNIT roles that made them famous.

Douglas Camfield
> *Walter Randall, Ian Fairbairn, Bruce Wightman, Geoffrey Cheshire, Michael Guest (including one non-speaking role, and his first work with Camfield when he was floor manager on* **Marco Polo**), *Sheila Dunn (Camfield's wife).*

Christopher Barry
> *Edward Kelsey (first cast by Barry in* **The Romans**, *followed by* **The Power of the Daleks** *and* **The Creature from the Pit**).

Derek Martinus
> *Roy Skelton (Skelton had worked on* **Doctor Who** *before as a voice artist, but Martinus just happened to direct a string of stories which required his kind of vocal talents – as Cybermen, Daleks, and the computer in* **The Ice Warriors**).

Michael Ferguson
> *Ric Felgate (and several others appearing twice for him, but he only directed four stories).*

Barry Letts
> *Christopher Burgess, Andrew Staines (and again, several others making only two appearances).*

David Maloney
> *Bernard Horsfall, Roy Skelton (Skelton, again, just happened to be the flavour of the month as, mainly, Dalek voices). Again, several others make two appearances in* **Doctor Who** *for him.*

Lennie Mayne
> *Rex Robinson. Several other artists appear more than once for Mayne in* **Doctor Who**, *not least because of his directing both Peladon stories.*

NARRATIVE

OH MY PROPHETIC SOUL
THE MASTER'S ESCAPES

It was in the nature of the Holmes/Moriarty relationship of the Third Doctor and the Master that the Doctor – and the audience – was always aware that the Master had escaped at the end of the story. In **The Mind of Evil**, the Master even rings up UNIT at Stangmoor Prison to make sure the Doctor knows he's safe (as an aside, it is interesting the note that while the Doctor has often protested that his police call box does not contain a telephone, the Master's TARDIS does!). But with later Doctors and Masters, the fact that the Master might have escaped from their previous encounter seems to come as something of a surprise. This is a list of stories in which the Doctor is openly surprised to find that the Master has escaped from their previous encounter. We do not include instances of the Doctor hoping that the Master has not escaped their previous encounter (like **Claws of Axos/Colony in Space**)

Logopolis
'He did escape from Traken,' the Doctor exclaims in surprise when he sees the miniaturised corpses of a policeman and Tegan's aunt in the back of her car.

Timeflight
'So you did escape from Castrovalva,' the Doctor exclaims in surprise as Khalid is revealed to be the Master.

The King's Demons
'You escaped from Xeraphas,' the Doctor exclaims in surprise as the anagramatic nature of Sir Giles Estram turns out to be no coincidence. As the Master replies, 'Oh my dear Doctor, you have been naive.'

Doctor Who: The Movie
For once, the Doctor does not seem to be at all surprised that the Master has escaped and is after him. Since he was spectacularly executed by the Daleks even before the opening credits, this is a very restrained attitude.

WELL, NOW WE'VE SOLVED IT

Unexplained phenomena are not always so unexplained in **Doctor Who**. In **Underworld** the Doctor hints that myths of the past may actually be prophecies of the future. Other instances are more explicit.

Occult stuff and black magic
*In **The Daemons** we discover that this is all the residual psionic science of the alien Daemons. Also, horns as a symbol of power in Earth mythology are a Daemon influence.*

Ghosts
*In **Image of the Fendahl** the Doctor remarks that haunted places are often near a time fissures, which is why they are haunted.*

Mary Celeste
*In **The Chase**, the appearance of the Daleks is enough to frighten crew and passengers into abandoning ship.*

Standing stones
*Some, at least, may be Ogri — silicon-based life forms from Ogros imprisoned on Earth as part of the stone circle named The Nine Travellers in **The Stones of Blood**.*

Impossible architecture
*Exxilon carvings in **Death to the Daleks** suggest the Exxilons' ancestors taught the inhabitants of ancient Peru how to build their temples.*

Egyptian mythology
*Ancient Egyptian culture, we are told in **Pyramids of Mars**, is based on the history of the Osirans. Horus defeated his brother Sutekh in Egypt and the wars of the gods passed into mythology.*

Abominable Snowmen
*Robot yeti controlled by the Great Intelligence terrorise the Himalayas in **The Abominable Snowmen**, and take to the London Underground in **The Web of Fear**. But just to show that not everything is as mundane as alien robots, we do do catch a glimpse of a real yeti at the end of **The Abominable Snowmen**.*

The Loch Ness Monster
*Nessie is either a cyborg creature brought to Earth by the Zygons in **Terror of the Zygons**, or the Borad, an alien scientist suffering from being accidentally half-reptile in **Timelash**. Or both, which could explain inconsistencies between sightings.*

Vampires
*In **State of Decay** we learn that there are vampire legends on almost every civilised world – all derived from the Great Vampires that Rassilon and the Time Lords defeated.*

The origins of life
*In **City of Death** a Jagaroth spaceship explodes and imbues the primordial soup with the energy it needs for life to start.*

Extinction of the dinosaurs
*Wiped out by the dust thrown up from the exploding space freighter carelessly sent back in time by the Cybermen to crash on to the Earth in **Earthshock**.*

Human development
*Both the Daemons (**The Daemons**) and Scaroth (**City of Death**) are said to have influenced development. So did the Rani, in fomenting unrest with her experiments (**Mark of the Rani**), and the Nemesis statue, with its baleful influence returning near Earth every twenty-five years (**Silver Nemesis**). The Fendahl influenced human development so that humans evolved eventually into a suitable form for the creature to re-create itself (**Image of the Fendahl**).*

Explanations for the destruction of Atlantis
Strangely, there are three competing explanations:

- **The Underwater Menace** – *Atlantis is destroyed when Professor Zaroff's fiendish experiments go predictably wrong. Since the story is set in the future, Atlantis has already sunk but not been destroyed.*
- **The Daemons** – *Azal cautions the Master not to mess with him by warning, 'My race destroys its failures – remember Atlantis.'*
- **The Time Monster** – *Kronos, the chronovore, is unleashed by the Master and destroys Atlantis, 3000 years ago.*

SOMEONE... LIKE YOU

There have been many instances of doubles for people popping up, by accident or evil design. Here's a list of the occasions where Doctors and companions have been 'doubled' along with some of the other more significant doubles. For the record, in **Day of the Daleks** and **The Space Museum**, the Doctor and his companions meet themselves, not doubles. And the incredible similarities between Steven and Morton Dill (**The Chase**), Harry Sullivan and Andrews (**Carnival of Monsters**) and Barbara and Lexa (**Meglos**) are merely coincidences of casting. We are also not including clone races such as the Drahvins or the Sontarans.

The Androids of Tara
As well as the coincidence of Romana being a double for Princess Strella, there's also an android version of the Princess sent to kill Prince Reynart and an android version of Romana sent to kill the Doctor. Prince Reynart is also replaced by an android double.

Arc of Infinity
Omega uses the Doctor's physical form as a template for his own new body.

Black Orchid
Ann Talbot happens to be a spitting image for Nyssa of Traken. Well, most of the time. Watch out for the shots where their heights are rather at variance.

The Chase
The Daleks make a robot copy of the Doctor. It has the strange ability to look and sound exactly like either William Hartnell's Doctor or Edmund Warwick, who doubled for Hartnell in this story. But it can't tell Vicki from Susan.

The Massacre of St Bartholomew's Eve
The Abbot of Amboise looks exactly like the Doctor. Interestingly, while Steven mistakes the Abbot for the Doctor (in particular when the Abbot's dead body is dumped in the gutter), the Abbot and the Doctor never meet.

The Enemy of the World
The Doctor is close enough to a double for dictator Salamander for them both to impersonate each other from time to time.

Meglos
Meglos, a large cactus, imitates the Doctor as part of his fiendish plan.

The Android Invasion
Predictably there are loads of android doubles in this one – including an android Doctor, Sarah, RSM Benton, Harry Sullivan, Colonel Faraday and various other

villagers, soldiers and tracking station personnel. There are even android dogs (presumably), though whether they are doubles of real animals is never revealed.

Terror of the Zygons
The Zygons can change their form to match a bodyprint taken from a captive. They double for Harry Sullivan, the Duke of Forgill, the Caber and Sister Lamont.

The Faceless Ones
The Chameleons steal the identities and appearances of planeloads of humans. Polly gets copied along with various airport and airline personnel and Detective Inspector Crossland.

The Claws of Axos
CIA man Bill Filer is copied and replaced by Axos.

The Five Doctors
The Second Doctor and Brigadier see illusions of Jamie and Zoe, while the Third Doctor sees Liz Shaw and Mike Yates.

The Mind Robber
The Doctor sees Jamie and Zoe, bleached white, beckoning him out of the safety of the TARDIS.

Planet of Evil
Professor Sorenson, mutated into Anti-Man, is split into copies of himself by careless use of a neutron accelerator.

Horror of Fang Rock
The Rutan can shape shift and copies lighthouse-keeper Reuben.

The Invisible Enemy
The Doctor and Leela are cloned (using a variation of the Kilbracken technique).

Face of Evil
Computer Xoanon accidentally gets some of the Doctor's personality – including, on occasion, his voice.

The Stones of Blood
Romana sees Cessair of Diplos in the form of the Doctor at the end of part one. But for some reason, we don't.

Destiny of the Daleks
*Despite the Doctor's protests, Romana copies the form of Princess Astra from **The Armageddon Factor** when she regenerates.*

The Armageddon Factor

On the Shadow's station, the Doctor sees copies of himself and Romana.

The Leisure Hive

There are many copies of Pangol that turn out actually to be copies of the Doctor. And there are the copies of Pangol and the Doctor that get manipulated on the Recreation Generator's visidome.

Spearhead from Space

Auton copies of many important figures in this story. In particular, General Scobie opens the door to his copy before he is immobilised and sent to Madame Tussauds.

The King's Demons and Planet of Fire

Kamelion is a shape-copying robot. He variously assumes the forms of King John, Tegan, the Master and the Doctor (**The King's Demons**), The Master and Professor Howard Foster (**Planet of Fire**).

Resurrection of the Daleks

The Daleks use genetically engineered doubles such as Kiston and Stien as their henchmen. They also make copies of Colonel Archer, Sergeant Calder and several soldiers, as well as the Doctor, Tegan and Turlough. Whether Lytton is a double is not clear, but events in **Attack of the Cybermen** (and early drafts of the script) suggest he is not.

Time and the Rani

The Rani impersonates Mel. Not a great act, but enough Bonnie Langford-esque whining and red hair to deceive the convalescent Doctor (as well as her hench-thing Urak) for a while.

Silver Nemesis

The Nemesis statue, made of living metal, is modelled on Lady Peinforte.

The Pirate Planet

The Doctor projects an image of himself to deceive the Captain and avoid having to walk the plank.

Timelash

The Borad killed by the Doctor turns out to be a clone. There's no hint of this earlier, but it makes for a terrific finale. Or something.

Davros

Following the Borad's example in the immediately preceding story, Davros plays a similar trick on his would-be assassin Orcini in **Revelation of the Daleks**. Quite where Davros was hiding while everyone thought he was a bodiless head in a revolving tank is not clear.

STAR TREKKING

Considering the length of time both series have been running, there have been very few overt **Star Trek** references in **Doctor Who**.

- In **The Horns of Nimon**, *the Doctor complains that people are always pointing phasers at him.*

- *Warp drive is mentioned in several stories, such as* **Planet of the Spiders** *and* **Earthshock** *– in rehearsals for which Beryl Reid apparently claimed it was just off Regent Street.*

- *The Federation of* **The Curse of Peladon** *and* **The Monster of Peladon** *could easily be the Earth Federation from* **Star Trek**. *Mind you, so could the tyrannical right-wing organisation of* **Blake's 7**.

- *The transmat in* **The Ark in Space** *looks very like a Transporter from* **Star Trek**. *That said,* **Doctor Who** *had teleportation (matter dissemination) in* **The Daleks' Master Plan** *and Travelling Mat (which Jamie thinks is a magic carpet), or T-Mat, in* **The Seeds of Death**. *In* **The Brain of Morbius**, *the Doctor describes teleportation as 'quaint.'*

TRAVEL DOES BROADEN THE MIND

The Doctor's adventures on Earth have been largely in England. The Home Counties in particular seem susceptible to alien invasions and the machinations of mad scientists. But the Doctor has on occasion ventured to other countries. The programme has only ever been on location in Britain, France (**City of Death**, set in Paris), the Netherlands (**Arc of Infinity**, set in Amsterdam), Lanzarote (**Planet of Fire**, set in Lanzarote and the planet Sarn), Spain (**The Two Doctors**, set in and around Seville), and Canada (**Doctor Who: The Movie**, set in San Francisco). But here, in no particular order are the countries (other than England) the Doctor has been seen to visit through the magic of the television studio. The list does not include places the Doctor claims to have been in incidents we did not witness, like watching the charge of the Light Brigade (**The Evil of the Daleks**) or joining the Filipino army for their final advance on Reykjavik (**The Talons of Weng-Chiang**). Nor do we include places the audience sees but the Doctor never gets to (like Switzerland in **The Tenth Planet**).

- Wales – **The Green Death, Delta and the Bannermen**

- Turkey – **The Myth Makers**

- Egypt – **The Daleks' Master Plan, Pyramids of Mars**

- Scotland – **The Highlanders, Terror of the Zygons, Timelash**, and probably **The Ice Warriors**

- France – **The Reign of Terror, The Massacre, City of Death**

- Italy – **The Romans, The Masque of Mandragora, City of Death**

- Palestine – **The Crusade**

- USA – **The Chase, The Gunfighters, Doctor Who: The Movie**

- Spain – **The Two Doctors**

- Antarctica – **The Tenth Planet, The Seeds of Doom**

- The Netherlands – **Arc of Infinity**

- China – **Marco Polo**

- Afghanistan – **Marco Polo**

- Lanzarote – **Planet of Fire**

- Tibet – **The Abominable Snowmen**

- Mexico – **The Aztecs**
- Atlantis, in the Azores – **The Underwater Menace**
- Atlantis, in the Aegean – **The Time Monster**
- Australia – **The Enemy of the World**
- Ghana (most probably) – **The Chase**
- Hungary –**The Enemy of the World**
- International waters and airspace – **The Chase, The Faceless Ones, Time-Flight, Warriors of the Deep**

GEORGE AND MARGARET

The Celestial Toymaker was originally to include the two eponymous characters mentioned significantly (and continually) in Gerald Savory's play **George and Margaret**. In the play, they are never seen, arriving off-stage just as the curtain falls. In the event **The Celestial Toymaker** was rewritten, and they failed to appear on television either. Here are some other characters who are mentioned significantly but never make it to the screen.

The Captain of Davros's space station prison
*In **Resurrection of the Daleks**, everyone lives in fear of the Captain. But he is killed in the initial Dalek attack on the station, so we never get to meet him.*

Ping Cho's fiancé
*Marco Polo (in, you guessed it, **Marco Polo**) takes Ping Cho all the way to the court of Kublai Khan for her arranged marriage to an old nobleman. She, and we, are saved the embarrassing introductions as he's already died by the time she gets there.*

Arthur
***Battlefield** builds up to the climactic meeting of the Doctor, Morgaine and Arthur. Except that Arthur's dead, which rather scuppers the end of the story.*

King Peladon's Parents
*In particular, his mother 'the Earth woman' is talked about in **The Curse of Peladon**.*

Missing Persons
*People who have disappeared or died are often mentioned – good examples being the survey team in **Planet of Evil** (Egard Lumb has a 'tombstone' and Lorenzo, Goora Summers are mentioned) and the missing crew in **Kinda** (in particular, Roberts is mentioned by name, and has his name on one of the crew chairs in the dome).*

Logar
*A shining deity in **Planet of Fire**. Actually he was a guy in a spacesuit. Kamelion is mistaken for Logar, but the real Logar is never identified.*

Theron
*We learn about Theron's views on justice and about how he led the Argolin into a terrible war with the Foamasi in **The Leisure Hive**. He's long dead, of course, but we do get to see his helmet.*

Canon Smallwood
*In **The Daemons** we are told only that Canon Smallwood resigned and left Devils' End without saying goodbye to anyone. Since he has been succeeded by the Master, we can guess the end result if not the details of the illness that forced him to resign.*

Turlough's solicitor

And a very strange man he is too, we are told in **Mawdryn Undead**.

The Federator

In **Snakedance** *we hear much about Lon's father and Tanha's husband, the Federator.*

King John

King John himself never actually appears in **The Kings' Demons**.

Mrs Sylvest

The twins' mother never appears but is referred to in **The Twin Dilemma**.

Miro

Commander of the Thal expedition to Spiridon in **Planet of the Daleks***, Miro was killed when they landed. It is possible that it's Miro's body which the Thals have left propped up in the pilot's seat for no better reason other than to scare Jo Grant.*

WHAT A GOOD IDEA

Over the years, **Doctor Who** stories have been inspired by – or even based on – various other pieces of written or celluloid fiction. Here are some possible story sources.

The Romans
Some gags and cast members lifted from **Carry on Cleo***.*

Spearhead from Space
This time **Quatermass II** *may be the inspiration for a disembodied group intelligence landing on Earth in hollow meteorites.*

Planet of the Daleks
The return of Terry Nation to the programme also saw a return of many of the plot elements of his very first Dalek story.

The Androids of Tara
The set-up, the doubles and even the ambush at the summerhouse are all from Anthony Hope's Ruritanian romance **The Prisoner of Zenda***.*

Planet of Evil
The planet that becomes hostile at night and Sorenson's decent into anti-man, are pure **Doctor Jekyll and Mister Hyde***. The antimatter creature is based on the id monster of* **Forbidden Planet** *(which is itself superficially based on Shakespeare's* **The Tempest***).*

The Android Invasion
No prizes for spotting the **Invasion of the Body Snatchers** *references here – even down to the organic-looking pods the androids emerge from when they reach Earth.*

The Brain of Morbius
Originally intended to invert Mary Shelley's **Frankenstein** *so that a robot tried to create a man, what was eventually created in the studio was rather closer to the original.*

The Seeds of Doom
Lots of references here. The Antarctic opening is reminiscent of **The Thing from Another World***, while the man into plant scenario is a nod to* **The Quatermass Experiment***. Less obviously, there are elements of the* **Avengers** *episode* **The Man-Eater of Surrey Green** *and the !950s television series and subsequent film* **The Trollenberg Terror***.*

The Deadly Assassin
Writer Robert Holmes and producer Philip Hinchcliffe say this was based on the film

The Manchurian Candidate (itself based on Richard Condon's book). Apart from the possibility that the Doctor has been 'programmed' to kill his President, there are actually few parallels. It's closer to a JFK conspiracy story.

Robot
Writer Terrance Dicks acknowledges that **King Kong** *is the source for the Robot's growth into a giant, and also for its relationship with Sarah.*

Castrovalva
As the title suggests, Escher's artwork was an inspiration for the recursive occlusions that beset the disintegrating world of Castrovalva, as well as its name.

Black Orchid
The mad relative in the attic is an old favourite, with literary validation from **Jane Eyre**. *The Peter Cushing film* **The Ghoul** *uses it well too.*

The Robots of Death
This story is a terrific mixture of Asimov's Lij Bailey robot detective stories and Agatha Christie.

The Talons of Weng-Chiang
Another successful blend, this time of **The Phantom of the Opera**, *Sax Rohmer's Fu-Manchu tales and Sherlock Holmes. The BBC show* **The Good Old Days** *is the inspiration for Jago's alliterative introductory speeches at the music hall — a device actually invented by Leonard Sachs to make his role more interesting, and with no historical grounding whatsoever.*

Underworld
Based on the myth of Jason and the Argonauts and throbbing with classical references.

The Horns of Nimon
Another myth source — the story of Theseus and the Minotaur, which was referred to in **The Creature from the Pit** *several stories earlier, when the Doctor shows off his big ball of string.*

State of Decay
A good blend of the best bits from the Vampire genre.

Warriors' Gate
Some visual references to Cocteau's films **Orphée** *and* **La Belle et la Bête**.

Curse of Fenric
Not so obvious, but this story has many elements in common with the John Carpenter film **The Fog**.

'WE MEET AGAIN, DOCTOR'

Companions, by definition, hang around for multiple stories. But various other characters have turned up more than once during the course of the Doctor's travels (we have excluded UNIT regulars, like Corporal Bell).

- Borusa – **The Deadly Assassin, The Invasion of Time, Arc of Infinity, The Five Doctors.**

- Professor Travers – **The Abominable Snowmen, The Web of Fear.**

- The Castellan – **Arc of Infinity, The Five Doctors.**

- Alpha Centauri – **The Curse of Peladon, The Monster of Peladon.**

- Davros – **Genesis of the Daleks, Destiny of the Daleks, Resurrection of the Daleks, Revelation of the Daleks, Remembrance of the Daleks.**

- The Master – various stories.

- Omega – **The Three Doctors, Arc of Infinity.**

- The White Guardian – **The Ribos Operation, The Stones of Blood** – voice only; **Enlightenment.**

- The Black Guardian – **The Armageddon Factor, Mawdryn Undead, Terminus, Enlightenment.**

- Cyberleader – 'We meet again, Doctor,' the Cyberleader says in **Earthshock**. So, perhaps they do.

NOBODY EXPECTS...

Ever since their first dramatic entrance – as a waving sink plunger – it has been something of a tradition for the Daleks to make their first appearance in a story at the end of the first episode, even though everyone knows they're on the way. Even if they have already popped up in the episode, they often come back to reinforce the point (**The Chase**, **Day of the Daleks**, and others). These are the stories in which Daleks appear for the first time at the end of part one.

The Daleks
In fact just a sucker arm waved in front of the camera by one of the studio staff. History in the making!

The Dalek Invasion of Earth
This prompted letters from parents of disappointed children who sat through 24 minutes waiting for more than the fleeting glimpse of a Dalek rising from the Thames.

The Power of the Daleks
Hidden in a spaceship in suspended animation and covered in cobwebs.

The Evil of the Daleks
Another one where the title was a bit of a clue.

Planet of the Daleks
Even the Doctor is surprised in this one – despite the fact he followed the Daleks there in the first place.

Death to the Daleks
Refusing to be put off the scent by talk of the mysterious sealed city, most viewers probably managed to work out what was inside the cake-tin spaceship.

Genesis of the Daleks
Also our first glimpse of Davros.

Destiny of the Daleks
The Daleks smash through that wall with so much panache and noise that you don't realise there's no reason for them to have put it there in the first place. Apart from for effect, of course.

TO BE PERFECTLY FRANK, HERBERT

H.G. Wells has been an obvious inspiration for **Doctor Who**. But overt references are actually rare.

Timelash

The wimpy character Herbert turns out to be none other than the young H.G. Wells. He does not like cricket, and displays various other character traits that are at odds with the H.G. Wells of our own universe.

Frontier in Space

The Master amuses himself by reading **The War of the Worlds**.

Pyramids of Mars

'I say, it's like something by that novelist chap, Mr Wells,' exclaims Laurence Scarman when he enters the TARDIS.

Horror of Fang Rock

Colonel Skinsale claims to be 'well acquainted with the scientific romances of Mr Wells.'

Black Orchid

The Doctor mentions Wells. Sir Robert has heard of him.

Doctor Who: The Movie

The Doctor reads **The Time Machine**.

HISTORY IN THE MAKING

There have been several actual historical events precipitated by the Doctor (so much for his early protestations that one shouldn't meddle in history). There are various other events he mentions that we don't see. And various other events he prevents others from preventing.

- **The Great Fire of Rome**
  *The Doctor inadvertently gives Nero the idea in **The Romans**.*

- **The desertion of the *Mary Celeste***
  *The Daleks chase the Doctor to the ship and frighten off the crew and passengers in **The Chase**.*

- **The wooden horse of Troy**
  *This is the Doctor's plan in **The Myth Makers** – after several other less popular suggestions like catapulting soldiers over the walls of Troy.*

- **The destruction of Atlantis**
  *Shown both in **The Underwater Menace** and **The Time Monster**.*

- **The Great Fire of London**
  *Actually started by the Doctor when he defeats the Terileptils in **The Visitation**. So his throwaway comment to Sarah in **Pyramids of Mars** that he doesn't want to be blamed for starting a fire as he had 'enough of that in 1666' is either a joke, or an earlier incarnation was wrongly blamed for the Fifth Doctor's handiwork.*

- **The extinction of the dinosaurs**
  *Adric is more personally 'involved' than the Doctor as the freighter crashes into prehistoric Earth in **Earthshock**.*

- **The creation of life on Earth**
  The Doctor stops Scaroth from preventing the explosion that destroyed the Jagaroth spaceship back in prehistoric times, as without that blast no Earth lifeforms would ever have evolved.

JOHN SMITH AND THE COMMON MEN

The Doctor has had many aliases during his adventures. These include:

John Smith

*Jamie's imaginative choice of name for the unconscious Doctor in **The Wheel in Space** sticks. The Doctor himself uses it in **Spearhead from Space** and on and off from then. Most recently, Chang Lee gives John Smith as the name of the Seventh Doctor when he takes him to hospital in **Doctor Who: The Movie**.*

I.M. Foreman

*The name on the doors of the junkyard where the TARDIS is in **100,000 BC**. Since Susan is Susan Foreman at Coal Hill School, the Doctor may well be I.M. The similarity to I am for Man is coincidental, of course...*

Doctor Caligari

*Rather improbably, the Doctor identifies himself in **The Gunfighters** as Doctor Caligari. Even more improbably, his companions become Steven Regret and Miss Dodo Dupont, wizard of the ivory keys. Quite what was wrong with their real names is unclear.*

The Examiner

*Another title rather than a pseudonym, this time in **The Power of the Daleks**. And again, the Doctor is capitalising on a case of mistaken identity.*

Doktor von Wer

*In **The Highlanders**, the Doctor just happens to pick the German for 'Who' as his alias.*

Doctor Galloway

*The Doctor plays along with the name Waterfield has given Perry when he sends him to meet the Doctor in a coffee bar in **The Evil of the Daleks**.*

An Examiner from the War Office

*In **The War Games**.*

Chairman Delegate from Earth

*A snappy nomenclature from **The Curse of Peladon**, accompanying princess Josephine of TARDIS.*

The Great Wizard Qui Quae Quod

*Latin taken from a source other than a black mass forms the Doctor's alias to win over the villagers of Devil's End in **The Daemons**. Another coincidental play on 'Who'.*

An Ajak

*The Doctor picks up on Mandrel's assumption that he is an Ajak, and tells the Gatherer in **The Sun Makers**.*

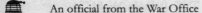

An official from the War Office

*In **The Curse of Fenric** the Doctor types out his own papers of authorisation and then forges the signatures of the Prime Minister and the head of the secret service on them – one with each hand.*

Galactic Insurance salesman

*The Doctor runs into a slight problem with his assumed identity as a representative of Galactic Insurance in **Nightmare of Eden** when it is pointed out to him that the company went bust many years previously. 'I wondered why I hadn't been paid,' he replies, aghast.*

IT IS I — THE DOCTOR

The Doctor has often had to disguise himself, either to get into somewhere, to get out again or, in extreme cases – like his milkman/cleaning-lady act in **The Green Death** – both.

Regional officer of the Provinces – **The Reign of Terror**

A Dalek exhibit – **The Space Museum**

The Monk – **The Time Meddler**

Zephon – **The Daleks' Masterplan**

Redcoat – **The Highlanders**

Washerwoman – **The Highlanders**

British soldier – **The Highlanders**

Gypsy – **The Underwater Menace**

Salamander – **The Enemy of the World**

The Karkus (sort of) – **The Mind Robber**

Alien student – **The War Games**

1917 British soldier specimen – **The War Games**

Technician in asbestos suit – **Inferno**

A Dalek – **Frontier in Space**

A Spiridon – **Planet of the Daleks**

Milkman – **The Green Death**

Cleaning-lady – **The Green Death**

Monk – **The Time Warrior**

A Thal guard – **Genesis of the Daleks**

An Osiran mummy – **Pyramids of Mars**

An android copy of himself – **The Android Invasion**

Chauffeur – **The Seeds of Doom**

Hieronymous – **The Masque of Mandragora**

A(nother) Time Lord – **The Deadly Assassin**

Levithian guard – **The Ribos Operation**

Pangol (sort of) – **The Leisure Hive**

Meglos – **Meglos**

Marine guard – **Warriors of the Deep**

NOTHING IN THE WORLD CAN STOP ME NOW!'

The Doctor has met more than his fair share of mad scientists over the centuries, though not all of them have been evil or even misguided. Consider the following extremists and eccentrics.

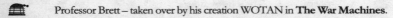

- Forrester – out to make a fortune at the expense of Earth's insect life in **Planet of Giants**.

- Professor Brett – taken over by his creation WOTAN in **The War Machines**.

- Lesterson – driven mad when he finds out the truth about the Daleks in **The Power of the Daleks**

- Professor Zaroff – the original 'Nothing in the world…' mad scientist in **The Underwater Menace**.

- Klieg – evil Logician out to revive the Cybermen from **The Tomb of the Cybermen**.

- Professor Travers – merely enthusiastic in **The Abominable Snowmen**, completely wacky forty years later in **The Web of Fear**.

- Professor Watkins – originally intended to be Travers again, but actor Jack Watling was unavailable for **The Invasion**.

- Professor Eldred – another aging eccentric in **The Seeds of Death**.

- Professor Stahlman – arrogant, confrontational and pretty single-minded even before he gets turned into a hairy monster in **Inferno**.

- Professor Jones – wacky ecologist who falls for Jo Grant, and later marries her, in **The Green Death**.

- Professor Rubeish – taken back to medieval times in his pyjamas (before Arthur Dent made such attire popular for galactic adventurers) in **The Time Warrior**.

- Professor Kettlewell – wacky creator of the K-1 robot in, of course, **Robot**.

- Davros – need we say more? He appeared in **Genesis of the Daleks**, **Destiny of the Daleks**, **Resurrection of the Daleks**, **Revelation of the**

Daleks and **Remembrance of the Daleks**.

Professor Sorenson – goes mad after being infected with antimatter in **Planet of Evil** (but becomes sane again later).

Mehendri Solon – out to create a new body to house **The Brain of Morbius**.

Taren Kapel – brought up by robots and out to 'liberate' them in **The Robots of Death**.

Magnus Greel – the so-called Butcher of Brisbane, responsible for killing many people during his experiments with a time cabinet, and transported back from the 51st century with a bent face for **The Talons of Weng-Chiang**.

Professor Nikolei Theodore Kerensky (and his time-travelling chickens) – in **City of Death**.

Soldeed – chief scientist of Skonnos, with a good line in ranting and raving in **The Horns of Nimon**.

Aukon – originally Science Officer O'Connor for the Hydrax, in **State of Decay**.

Sharaz Jek – has a consuming hatred of Morgus, the man who tried to kill him but only managed to leave him disfigured, in **The Caves of Androzani**.

The Rani – amoral renegade Time Lord scientist in **Mark of the Rani** and **Time and the Rani**.

Joynson Dastari – enhancer of Androgums and ally of the Sontarans in **The Two Doctors**.

The Borad – mutated remains of Karfellon scientist Magellan in **Timelash**.

Crozier – up to a spot of mind-transplanting in **The Trial of a Time Lord** (parts five to eight).

SORRY WE'RE LATE

Sometimes it just seems to take ages for the Doctor and his team to arrive on the scene, despite having a TARDIS to get them there. Here are some examples:

The Space Museum
Not strictly true, as in effect the Doctor, Ian, Barbara and Vicki have been there for ages, as exhibits in the museum. But it is not until the end of episode 1 that time, which has jumped a track and let the other forms of themselves see into their own future, gets back on course and the TARDIS team 'arrive.'

Mission to the Unknown and The Daleks' Master Plan
*Although the Doctor and co arrive at the start of **Master Plan**, events are already an episode along – and the Doctor didn't so much as get a look in for **Mission to the Unknown**.*

The Tenth Planet
Episode 1 is well underway before the TARDIS arrives at the South Pole.

The Green Death
Although the Brigadier and Jo head off to the trouble in Wales at the drop of a green body, the Doctor insists on taking a trip to Metebelis III first.

The Time Warrior
Linx arrives, sets up shop with Irongron and starts kidnapping scientists before the Doctor and Brigadier start wondering where they've gone.

The Monster of Peladon
Another story where the action is well-advanced before the TARDIS arrives, and dumps the Doctor (this time with Sarah) into the middle of a dicey situation.

Planet of the Spiders
They really made a feature of it this season. The focus is on Mike Yates and Sarah at the start of this story, and the two storylines – the meditation centre and the Doctor's experiments in precognition – take until part 2 to come together.

The Seeds of Doom
By the time the World Ecology Bureau decide to call for expert help, their survey team has dug up a Krynoid pod, thawed it out, send photos to London by satellite, got snowed in, had a game of three-handed crib, and had one of their party turn green and sprout shoots. No wonder the Doctor decides that short of amputation it's probably too late to help.

Meglos
Again, we see the Doctor, Romana and K-9 early on. But thanks to Meglos' nifty time loop, they do not arrive on Tigella, where the action is, until well into part 2.

Full Circle

Lots of necessary story exposition setting up Alzarius, Mist Fall, the Outlers, Adric and his brother, the Deciders and lots of other stuff before the Doctor, K-9 and Romana arrive to sort things out.

The Keeper of Traken

The Doctor and Adric, after getting chatted up by the Keeper, don't really turn up on Traken until nearly the end of part one.

Vengeance on Varos

Thanks to their inexplicable lack of spare supplies of Ziton ore, the Doctor and Peri mooch about in the TARDIS for a good part of episode 1 before managing to arrive on Varos. And then they wish they hadn't.

A MEGALOMANIAC MACHINE, BUT STILL A MACHINE

Mad computers are scientific nonsense, of course. Or are they? The Doctor has certainly encountered a few… That said, many of the computers (like Mentalis in **The Armageddon factor**) he has combatted have merely been following their programs.

WOTAN (Will Operating Thought ANalogue)
*A computer linked to a human brain, that of its creator Proffessor Brett, in **The War Machines**. Clever enough to work out the meaning of TARDIS, but thinks the Doctor's name is Doctor Who.*

The Boss (Bimorphic Operational Systems Supervisor)
*The first computer ever to be linked to a human brain, again. This time the brain belongs to the director of Global Chemicals, Stevens, in **The Green Death**.*

Xoanon
*Driven mad by a mind-link with the Doctor prior to the events of **Face of Evil**. Presumably, then, the first computer to be linked to a Time Lord brain (or was that the Matrix?).*

The Oracle
*The computer guarding the Minyan race banks. It gets above itself in **Underworld**.*

The M3 robot Drathro
*Didn't know what planet he was on in **The Trial of a Time Lord** (parts one to four)*

Sandminer robots
*Reprogrammed, or homocidal maniacs in **The Robots of Death**? SV7 and his colleagues are very calm about it either way ('Do not kill me').*

The K1 robot
*Driven mad when he accidentally kills his creator, Kettlewell, in **Robot**, the robot has already been rendered 'unwell' enough to kill people in contravention of his prime directive. The Doctor diagnoses 'suppressed Oedipus Complex' and, strangely for an intended cure, prescribes a metal virus.*

The superbrain that controls the Land of Fiction
*Not that we ever discover what the computer really was or where it came from in **The Mind Robber**. Its plans boiled down to an intended invasion of Earth though, with the intention of turning the inhabitants into sausages, according to the Doctor. Er, which one was mad?*

DOES YOUR CAILLEACH RIDE A BICYCLE?

Have you ever wondered how many bicycles have appeared in **Doctor Who**? So have we... so we just *had* to find out!

Shada
Lots of bicycles in Cambridge, not least the one the Doctor rides pursued by Skagra's sphere.

The Stones of Blood
'Does your Cailleach ride a bicycle?' the Doctor asks casually while tied to the sacrificial stone. The bicycle in question is ridden (well, pushed) by Professor Rumford.

Logopolis
The unfortunate policeman in the opening sequence has a bike. The bicycle falls from its position leaning against the police box when the Master's TARDIS materialises. Adric uses the bike to help the Doctor escape the police later.

The Daemons
One of the villagers in the background has a bicycle during the revels on the village green. Local bobby, PC Groom is about to get on his bike when he meets Miss Hawthorne.

Arc of Infinity
There are a lot of bicycles knocking about in Amsterdam in the background. The publicity stills for the story (and the female companions' new costumes) feature a bicycle made for three, but this never features in the story.

The Claws of Axos
Pigbin Josh finds a battered bike, but does not live long enough to enjoy it much.

Spearhead from Space
One of the shop window Autons' victims is riding a bicycle when he is targeted.

The War Machines
An arty shot of a bicycle in a puddle as a War Machine is reflected passing by.

Mawdryn Undead
Turlough and Ibbotson narrowly miss a cyclist on their joyride in the Brigadier's car.

Image of the Fendahl
Ted Moss has a bicycle when he is waylaid by Leela.

The Daleks' Master Plan
The 'Man in Mackintosh' clutches one.

Inferno
Harry Slocum rides a bicycle to the drill head in the opening sequence.

The Space Museum
Under interrogation by Lobos, the wily Doctor projects a picture of a penny-farthing onto a mind-monitoring device's screen when asked how he arrived.

The Greatest Show in the Galaxy
The Whizz Kid has a really neat racy bike just like we – er, no, nothing like we ever dreamed of. Or even wanted, come to that.

PRAISE THE COMPANY

Just some of the fictitious establishments the Doctor has had dealings with or referred to.

Global Chemicals
*Strangely, renamed from Universal Chemicals in the original script, and then changed to Panorama Chemicals for the novelisation of **The Green Death**.*

Chameleon Tours
*An airline that takes you further than you might guess in **The Faceless Ones**.*

Interplanetary Mining Corporation
*The bad guys in **Colony in Space**.*

The Company
*Running things in **The Sun Makers** – maybe Usurians are short on imagination...*

The Company
*Running the Sandminers back in Kaldor City in **The Robots of Death** – maybe these fat cats are also short on imagination.*

The Company
*Running the refinery in **The Power of Kroll** – they get about, don't they?*

I.M. Foreman
*Possibly a scrap merchant in **100,000 BC** and **Remembrance of the Daleks**.*

London Television
*The company Harold Chorley works for in **The Web of Fear***

Eurogas
*In **Fury from the Deep**.*

International Electromatics
*Tobias Vaughn's sinister outfit in **The Invasion**.*

Issigri Mining Corporation
*In **The Space Pirates**.*

Hibernian Oil Co. Ltd.
*Hard hit by the Skarasen's antics in **Terror of the Zygons**.*

Laserson
*It appears to be a trademark in **The Robots of Death**.*

The Leisure Hive
*It's a commercial concern in, unsurprsingly, **The Leisure Hive**.*

Morgus's unnamed company
*In **The Caves of Androzani**.*

Comtech Division
*Markets the video nasties in **Vengeance on Varos**.*

Galatron Mining Corporation
*Sil's company in **Vengeance on Varos**.*

Tranquil Repose
*Dead dodgy in **Revelation of the Daleks**.*

The Fantasy Factory
*A nightmare to run in **The Trial of a Time Lord** (parts thirteen to fourteen).*

Nostalgia Tours
*Intergalactic holiday outfit in **Delta and the Bannermen**.*

Ratcliffe Builder's Merchants
*Personnel and premises both took a battering in **Remembrance of the Daleks**.*

The Psychic Circus
*Sinister set-up for the Gods of Ragnorok in **The Greatest Show in the Galaxy**.*

Eternity Perpetual Company
*Made everlasting power supplies, and hence went out of business, we learn in **Carnival of Monsters**.*

Auto Plastics
*Under Nestene management in **Spearhead from Space**.*

Farrels
*Ditto in **Terror of the Autons**.*

Terminus Inc
*Sloppy customer treatment in **Terminus**.*

Emmett's Electronics
*In **Robot**.*

Galactic Insurance
*Sadly out of business by the time of the **Nightmare of Eden**.*

Hayhoe Launderers Co. and Silcock Bakeries
*Actually supposed to be fictitious companies in **The Ambassadors of Death**.*

QUITE THE MASTER CRIMINAL

Despite his good intentions, the Doctor has actually committed many crimes. Consider how he might defend himself against the following, for example:

Stealing a TARDIS
*Implied in various stories, and explicitly stated at times, for example in **Planet of the Spiders**.*

Stealing a car
***Spearhead from Space**, **The Seeds of Doom** – though in the latter case he might argue he was returning it.*

Damage to property
On countless occasions.

Stealing clothes
*In **The Crusade**, **Spearhead from Space**, **Doctor Who: The Movie**…*

Grievous bodily harm
*Numerous occasions, especially in the Pertwee era, but also **The Reign of Terror**, where he hits a roadworks overseer over the head with a spade; **The Romans** where he beats up a mute assassin; **The Seeds of Doom** where he duffs up Chase's chauffeur, and numerous assaults on aliens and monsters.*

Impersonation
*In **The Power of the Daleks**, **The Highlanders**, **The Curse of Peladon**, **Nightmare of Eden**; numerous others.*

Disobeying orders
*Again, many examples, but especially **Inferno** and **The Green Death**.*

Resisting arrest
*When doesn't he? Notable examples include **Invasion of the Dinosaurs** and **Logopolis**.*

Speeding
*Again, where to start? How about the superdrive sequences in **The Time Monster**, and most of part two of **Planet of the Spiders**…?*

Desecrating a holy place
***The Curse of Peladon**, **The Monster of Peladon**, and others*

Breaking and entering
Far, far too many to list!

Genocide
The Trial of a Time Lord (not proven), plus attempts in Genesis of the Daleks, The Sea Devils, The Evil of the Daleks, and arguably in Pyramids of Mars where he kills the last Osiran. And others!

Forgery
Of signatures, for example, in The Curse of Fenric.

Drunk and disorderly
Reported only, and apparently involving lots of drink and a fountain — his spree with Azmael is referred to in The Twin Dilemma.

Sedition
The Happiness Patrol to name but one…

Theft
Again, too many instances to list including stealing bits of the Monk's and Master's TARDISes over the years. Most recent is his pilfering of a beryllium chip from Professor Wagg's atomic clock in Doctor Who: The Movie.

TRIALS OF THE TIME LORDS

Not only have the Time Lords put their own people on trial, they've had up others too. And Time Lords have on occasion been tried by other courts…

The War Games
Not only is the Doctor put on trial by the Time Lords for his crimes, but so is the War Lord. The Doctor is also court martialled in the 1917 time zone.

The Sea Devils
References back to the Master's trial following his capture at the end of **The Daemons**. *Apparently, he narrowly escaped the death sentence, for which he thanks the Doctor.*

The Brain of Morbius
Morbius, we learn, was tried by the Time Lords and vapourised. Somehow, of course, they overlooked his brain.

The Deadly Assassin
The Doctor on trial on Gallifrey again, this time for assassinating the president. The trial never concludes as the Doctor offers himself as a candidate for the presidency and so must be freed to make his election pitch. Of course, since he is the only candidate left standing at the end of the story he accidentally wins. The trial is never concluded.

The Stones of Blood
The Megara, justice machines with some organic componentry, try the Doctor for breaking the seals on their travel compartment. He defends himself, and calls Romana, Vivien Fay and the Megara themselves as witnesses.

The Leisure Hive
The Doctor is arrested for the murder of Stimson, who was strangled with the Doctor's scarf. His 'trial' is to test out the Recreation Generator – which unfortunately ages him 500 years.

Arc of Infinity
This time the Time Lords dispense with a trial altogether, not surprising since the Doctor is not actually accused of any crime. They just skip straight to the 'execution by vaporisation' bit…

The Trial of a Time Lord
Bit of an obvious one, really.

Doctor Who: The Movie
The Master is executed for his crimes by the Daleks. Whether there was actually a trial or not is unclear. Knowing the Daleks, probably not.

ANNO DOMINI, DOCTOR

Dating some of the **Doctor Who** stories can be problematic. The UNIT stories in particular are elusive, not least because of the contradiction between Sarah's claim to be from 1980, and the setting of the Brigadier's retirement (in **Mawdryn Undead**) before 1977. But here are the stories which are definitely set in the present (give or take a year or two). We have assumed that the UNIT stories were actually set, as the production team of the time intended, in the near future, which ties in with the date Sarah gives in **Pyramids of Mars**. We have ignored minor quibbles like the fact that the taxi diver in **Doctor Who and the Silurians** was paid in shillings and pence – who knows when decimalisation actually arrived in the **Doctor Who** universe?

An Unearthly Child
Susan says 'We've left 1963…'.

Planet of Giants
So far as one can tell – it needs to be contemporary with **An Unearthly Child** for the irony to work

The Chase
Just the end, where Barbara and Ian return home to find bus fares have increased.

The Massacre of St Bartholomew's Eve
Only the very end only where Dodo joins the TARDIS crew.

The War Machines
Although they get the days of the week wrong!

The Faceless Ones
*Almost. It is set immediately following **The War Machines** – a year before the story was transmitted.*

The Evil of the Daleks
*Opening episode and first half of part 2 immediately follow **The Faceless Ones**, so are set in the year prior to transmission.*

Image of the Fendahl
According to the BBC trailer the previous week.

City of Death
1979 – the vintage of which is 'more of a table wine'.

Shada
Probably.

Logopolis
The date is confirmed in **The Visitation**.

Four to Doomsday

Time-Flight

Arc of Infinity

Mawdryn Undead
Just the present day bits, obviously.

The Awakening
Tegan's relative doesn't seem surprised at her apparent age, and we are told how long ago the civil war battle was.

Resurrection of the Daleks
Given the date for **Attack of the Cybermen**, *and the continuity of Lytton's involvement in both.*

Attack of the Cybermen

The Two Doctors
Apparently.

Silver Nemesis

Survival
Given the fact that Ace fits back in with her Perivale gang without an age problem.

ALSO KNOWN AS . . .

It isn't only the Doctor and the Master who use pseudonyms. Here are some other examples of people who are not quite who they claim.

Ace
Real name Dorothy. Surname not known although her mother's maiden name was Dudman.

Steven Regret
*Steven Taylor's pseudonym in **The Gunfighters**. Not clear why he couldn't use his real name.*

Dodo Dupont
*Dodo's pseudonym in **The Gunfighters**. Again, it's not clear what was wrong with her real name...*

Michelle Leuppi
*Psuedonym used by the Cameleon with Polly's form in **The Faceless Ones**.*

Cressida
*Actually Vicki in **The Myth Makers**.*

The Great Healer
*Davros in **Revelation of the Daleks**.*

Dask
*Identity assumed by Taren Kapel in **The Robots of Death**. It isn't clear what happened to the real Dask if there was one.*

D84
*Since he can talk he can't really be a Dum (D-class) robot. Presumably he's actually a Super Voc (SV-class) in **The Robots of Death**.*

Josiah Samuel Smith
*The experiment in **Ghost Light**. We never learn his 'real' name if he has one.*

Count Scarlioni
*One of the splinters of Scaroth in **City of Death**.*

Captain Tancredi
Another of Scaroth's splinters.

Noah
*Nickname for Lasar, commander of **The Ark in Space**.*

Weng-Chiang -

Assumed name of Magnus Greel in **The Talons of Weng-Chiang** *(itself a name-change from* **The Talons of Greel**).

Grenville
Cover name for Hallett in **The Trial of a Time Lord** *(parts nine to eleven).*

Enzu
Cover name for Hallett when he's posing as a Mogarian. How many passports does this guy have?

Nurse
A profession rather than a name for the young projection of Queen Xanxia in **The Pirate Planet**.

Vivian Fay, Mrs Trefusis, Senhora Camara, Lady Montcalm
Names assumed through the ages by Cessair of Diplos during her time on Earth in **The Stones of Blood**. *In her spare time she is also the Calleach, Nermentana, Kerrywing and others.*

Aukon
One of the original crew of the Hydrax. Apart from becoming an immortal vampire for **State of Decay**, *his name underwent a consonantal shift from (Anthony) O'Connor (science officer).*

Zargo
Captain of the Hydrax, originally Miles Sharkey.

Camilla
Another one from the Hydrax, originally she was Lauren Macmillan (navigational officer).

Edgeworth
An assumed name for Time Lord Azmael, the reason for which is never explained, in **The Twin Dilemma**.

The Borad
A title really, but it does conceal the identity of misguided (and mutated) scientist Magellan in **Timelash**.

J.J.Chambers, Mr Popplewick
Are both (or rather all, since there are several Popplewicks of various ages) the Valeyard in the final parts of **The Trial of a Time Lord**. *And the Valeyard is, of course, the Doctor — well, sort of.*

People who have pretended to be the Doctor

Here are a few who have assumed the identity of the Doctor for one reason or another:

Salamander
Seems fair enough, since the Doctor spends odd moments in **The Enemy of the World** *pretending to be Salamander.*

Cessair of Diplos
We hear her impression of the Doctor in **The Stones of Blood**, *but never actually see it. It's good enough to frighten Romana into backing off a cliff, though.*

Meglos
A good likeness. At least, till he goes green and comes out in spikes.

Mawdryn
Not a great performance. How do Tegan, Nyssa and the Brig fall for this in **Mawdryn Undead**? *It's a piece of cake, it seems — just put on the coat, and pretend you're the Doctor with a plate of spaghetti on his head.*

QUICK — THE PLOT DEVICE!

The temptation for a quick deus-ex-machina to wrap up the story is sometimes just too great for both the Doctor and the script writer. Here are just some of the more outrageous examples from the programme's history.

The Daleks

In the original storyline, an alien race arrived at the end of the story to say that they were responsible for the Thal-Dalek war all those years ago, and now they're very sorry and what can they do to help. Imagine the problems with later Dalek stories if they had all patched up their differences and lived happily ever after… Thank goodness the ending was changed to a good old battle to the death.

The Web Planet

An Isop-tope cell destructor? Lucky the Menoptra brought that with them. Very handy for, well, for destroying the Animus in a couple of episodes' time, no doubt.

The Daleks' Master Plan

It's amazing really that it takes until episode 12 for the Doctor to realise that the Taranium core he's been running around with all this time is the vital component for an awesome weapon – a Time Destructor, no less – that could just be the answer to his problems.

The Ark

Here we are on Refusis at last. What luck that the local highly-advanced invisible life form is waiting to sort out the difficulties between humans and Monoids that have plagued the last four episodes.

The War Games

Big problem – all those humans stuck on a nameless planet thinking they're fighting wars from earth's history. How will the Doctor sort out the War Lord and get them home? Easy, for one story only (and forget previous little problems with Daleks, Cybermen, Yeti, Ice Warriors and the like) we'll send for the Time Lords.

The Mutants

What luck – Ky isn't ill at all, he's just turned into a super-intelligent life form and sorted everything out for us. Phew.

The Time Monster

At the end of the story, Kronos the chronovore who's been generally unpleasant the whole way through turns out to be a big softy. She puts everything (well, nearly everything) right, and even lets the Master go rather than take revenge.

The Green Death

Another amazing coincidence here – imagine the chances of the fungus they cultivate (breed?) at the nuthutch happening to be exactly the biological counter-strike they need for the oil waste and resulting mutant maggots. It'll even cure the disease and sort out your dandruff too. Who says life is stranger than fiction?

The Hand of Fear
Good old King Rokon – he sorted it all out millions of years ago. Kind of him to leave a video telling us about it.

The Invasion of Time
How lucky that the great secret that the Doctor now knows and is able to impart to Rodan and K-9 is how to construct the De-mat Gun – a terrible secret weapon. OK, so it's banned by the Time Lords, but it's a whizz for stopping alien invasions in episode 6.

Arc of Infinity
Oh no, Doctor, we can't possibly not kill you – there's no way we could stop Omega. But surely, the Doctor retorts, if I just snap together these bits of plastic into a sort of sparkler gun thing and shoot him…

The Five Doctors
Rassilon, Time Lord hero who's been dead for centuries, pops up to save the day. Another close call there.

Warriors of the Deep
Hardly deus ex machina, *more a case of* deus obviousa*! As soon as someone mentions that the masses of Hexachromite on Seabase 4 will destroy all reptile life, we just begin to get an inkling of where this might be leading…*

Attack of the Cybermen
Handy Vastial (from the same company that brought you Hexachromite, no doubt) just happens to explode when it's above freezing point. And the Cybermen have carelessly locked up the Doctor and chum in a room full of the stuff.

The Trial of a Time Lord (parts five to eight)
How to get the Doctor out of a tricky situation? Why not have the Time Lords turn up and whisk him away?

Silver Nemesis
*The Doctor spends the whole story trying to stop the Nemesis from becoming complete just to draw out the suspense until part 3 when it becomes whole and wipes out the Cyber fleet. A neat trick, but several points deducted for having tried exactly the same move against the Daleks two stories back (in **Remembrance of the Daleks**).*

Doctor Who: The Movie
*It's not really clear what a temporal orbit is, or what Grace or the Doctor do with the TARDIS. But whatever it is, it puts everything right, makes everyone better, and breaks several cardinal rules of time, **Doctor Who**, and script writing.*

IS IT REALLY YOU?

It's only happened a few times, but there have been occasions where beings have appeared in **Doctor Who** actually playing themselves.

K-9
*OK, so John Leeson and David Brierley provided the voice (**The Invisible Enemy to Warriors' Gate**, plus **K-9 and Company: A Girl's Best Friend**).*

Kamelion
*Who also, of course, appeared as various other people (**The King's Demons, Planet of Fire**).*

The Beatles
*In their promo-film of 'Ticket to Ride' in **The Chase**.*

Kenneth Kendal
*As his news-reading self in **The War Machines**, keeping us up to date on the WOTAN crisis.*

Alex MacIntosh
*The news reporter (named in the caption) at Auderly House when the peace conference starts in **Day of the Daleks** who was a news presenter.*

The Cambridge Choristers
*Singing their hearts out as the Doctor whizzes past in **Shada**.*

Courtney Pine
*The famous jazz personality appears as himself playing in a pub garden in **Silver Nemesis**. Ace asks for, and gets, his autograph.*

ALL HE DOES IS CAUSE TROUBLE

The Master has committed countless crimes over the millennia. Here are some of the more blatant ones we actually know about:

- **Murder by miniaturisation**
  Countless occasions, particularly, **Terror of the Autons**, **The Deadly Assassin**, **Logopolis**…

- **Murder by other means**
  Too many to enumerate, but including by daffodil and by armchair in **Terror of the Autons**.

- **Attempted murder**
  For example, by telephone cord in **Terror of the Autons**.

- **Misuse of a radio telescope**
  In both **Terror of the Autons** *and* **Logopolis**.

- **Phone-tapping**
  In **The Mind of Evil**.

- **Supplying weapons**
  To the prisoners at Stangmoor in **The Mind of Evil**.

- **Careless driving**
  Once again, in **The Mind of Evil**.

- **Assassination**
  Or attempted assassination anyway, on numerous occasions, notably **The Deadly Assassin**.

- **Forgery**
  Of ID and papers as Adjudicator (**Colony in Space**), Police Commissioner (**Frontier in Space**), and so on.

- **Blackmail**
  Not least, holding the universe to ransom in **Logopolis**.

- **Aiding and abetting an alien invasion force**
  Examples include the Nestenes in **Terror of the Autons**, *Axos in* **The Claws of Axos**, *the Daleks in* **Frontier in Space**…

- **Hypnotism**
  Tell us about it.

Impersonation
Of an army officer priest/Adjudicator/naval officer/police commissioner and others.

Kidnapping and hostage-taking
*From **Terror of the Autons** onwards, really.*

Escaping from custody
*Particularly in **The Sea Devils**.*

Resisting arrest
*For example, in **The Daemons**.*

Theft
*He's stolen just about everything from spaceships (**Frontier in Space** and others) to hovercraft (**The Sea Devils**), from information held in the Time Lord Files (**Colony in Space**, **The Sea Devils**) to a Concorde (**Time-Flight**).*

Adultery
*Oo-er. Heavy implications of this with Queen Galleia in **The Time Monster**.*

Illegal access to the Matrix and APC-Net
*To get Time Lord secrets in **The Deadly Assassin** and **The Trial of a Time Lord**.*

Moving innocent people through time without permission
*Like civil war roundhead soldiers and a knight on horseback in **The Time Monster**.*

Upsetting the Daleks
*This got him executed in **Doctor Who: The Movie**. Perhaps his cock-up in **Frontier in Space** finally caught up with him?*

MEN OUT THERE ARE DYING FOR IT

Incredibly, believe it or not, there have been some stories where nobody actually dies!

- **Inside the Spaceship**

- **The Celestial Toymaker**
  We assume the Toymaker does not actually die at the end, he is said to be immortal.

- **The Savages**

- **Fury from the Deep**

- **The Mind Robber**

- **Castrovalva**
  Well, nobody real dies.

- **Four to Doomsday**

- **Snakedance**

NO CHANGE THERE

Although some of the Doctor's companions have changed their clothes at every opportunity to exploit the latest in 'high fashion' (often misguidedly), others have not. Jo Grant must hold the record for most conscientious companion in the former category, unless we count Sarah's late rally in **K-9 and Company: A Girl's Best Friend** (four changes of clothing in the opening titles alone). But here, in ascending order of 'whiff' are those individuals who have not worried quite so much about keeping a clean pair of socks handy.

The Doctor
*Maybe he has a Time Lord perspiratory bypass system, but we rarely see the Doctor wash – the odd shower (**Spearhead from Space**), enforced cleansing (**The Macra Terror**), and the occasional bath (**Black Orchid** – if he ever gets round to having it!). And most of the time he's in pretty much the same togs for a whole incarnation. Particularly unchanged are the second, fifth and sixth Doctors – the others swap coats, capes, and frilly shirts now and again.*

The Master
*Same excuse as the Doctor, presumably. There is some variation in the black suits, though. And by **Doctor Who: The Movie** he has become so clothes conscious that he slips away to change into full Time Lord gear in time for the finale – 'I always dress for the occasion.'*

UNIT personnel
*There is some change, with smart new uniforms for **Spearhead from Space** (cf **The Invasion**) and **Terror of the Autons** in particular. Benton sports a nice jumper under his tunic in **The Ambassadors of Death**, and all the regulars get a change at some point in **The Daemons**. One hopes the UNIT budget runs to more than a single uniform per soldier too.*

Ace
*Some variations on the leggings-and-bomber-jacket theme, and she washes her hair in **Remembrance of the Daleks**.*

Davros
Well, maybe he has several of those nice shiny black tunics, with special buttons that are easy to do up with one hand while sitting down…

Nyssa
Gets off to a slow start, reluctant to change out of that velvet Traken jacket (though the skirt is soon replaced by practical adventuring trousers). But by the time she leaves in

Terminus, she can't wait to change clothes at the drop of a skirt...

Leela

*Owing to the variation in recording order and transmission order of some of her stories, Leela seems to change into a new leather outfit for **Image of the Fendahl**, back again for **The Sun Makers**, and into the new outfit again for **Underworld**. She also sports clothes of the era for **The Talons of Weng-Chiang** and **Horror of Fang Rock**. In fact, the most time she spends apparently in the same togs is just 10 episodes (**Underworld** and **The Invasion of Time**).*

Tegan

*It's difficult to find any mitigating circumstances for Tegan's insistence on wearing a purple airline outfit for **Logopolis, Castrovalva, Four to Doomsday, Kinda, Earthshock** and **Time-Flight**. Let's hope she used the short breaks (when she's asleep in **Castrovalva**, and dolled up for the party in **Black Orchid**) to get the thing dry cleaned.*

Jamie

*Pretty much the same clothes, with the odd lapse (like a guard's uniform for part of The **Enemy of the World** and the occasional polo-neck sweater) from **The Highlanders** to **The War Games**. His excuse being, presumably, that people in 1746 Scotland didn't change clothes a lot anyway. One almost hopes he doesn't wear anything under his kilt.*

Adric

*Only ever changed out of his pyjama-outfit (and possibly had a bath, though there is no evidence to support this theory) for the party in **Black Orchid**, and was straight back into it for **Earthshock**. His only documented bath was a dip in the Alzarian river to steal some river fruits in **Full Circle**.*

SLEEP IS FOR TORTOISES

While the Doctor may not seem to appreciate sleep, there are many occasions when he or his companions are seen to grab forty winks or more...

100,000 BC
Some kip is grabbed in the Cave of Skulls.

Inside the Spaceship
Everyone needs a good rest in this one. Ian sleepwalks.

The Keys of Marinus
The Doctor and companions all sleep. Bad move.

The Dalek Invasion of Earth
The Doctor, weakened by the robotisation process, collapsesand spends episode 4 unconscious.

The Rescue
The Doctor is asleep when the TARDIS lands.

The Web Planet
Vicki tries to sleep off her headache.

The Crusade
Ian sleeps in the desert. Bad move.

The Chase
The TARDIS crew sleep in a cave on Mechanus, and are observed by a surveillance camera.

The Time Meddler
The Doctor sleeps overnight in his cell in the monastery, and when the Monk wakes him, violently refuses his breakfast.

The Massacre of St. Bartholomew's Eve
The story covers four days, and Steven has to find somewhere to sleep for three nights. So does Anne — oo-er.

The War Machines
The Doctor spends the night at Sir Charles Summer's house.

The Tenth Planet
The Doctor collapses at the beginning of episode 3, and sleeps through it. He also conks out in the Cyberman spaceship.

The Moonbase
Jamie is concussed and sleeps it off in the sick bay, only to be confronted by the Phantom Piper.

The Macra Terror
The Doctor and companions all sleep. Bad move.

The Tomb of the Cybermen
Doctor, companions and archaeology team grab some sleep in the Cyber city. Bad move.

The Wheel in Space
The Doctor is concussed and spends episode 2 asleep

The Mind Robber
Jamie falls asleep in the TARDIS console room and dreams of unicorns. Did he dream the whole thing?

The Invasion
Jamie sleeps while the Doctor works at Watkins' house in episode six.

The Seeds of Death
Once more the Doctor is unconscious for an episode…

The War Games
Jamie and Zoe go to sleep in the chateau and are rudely awoken by Arturo Villar's arrival.

Spearhead from Space
The Doctor rests at Ashbridge Cottage Hospital after his enforced regeneration. The Doctor also sleeps after his wounding at the end of episode 1.

The Mind of Evil
After his ordeal with the Keller machine, the Doctor sleeps it off in his cell. The Brigadier is also found asleep at his desk by the Doctor and Chin Lee.

The Daemons
The Doctor is in a coma for a while, Jo gets knocked out and needs sleep, and the Brigadier wakes to find Yates and Benton have gone off in his helicopter.

Day of the Daleks
Jo falls asleep on the ghostwatch. She wakes to find nothing has happened.

The Time Monster
Opens with the Doctor's precognitive nightmare about the Master and the Crystal of Kronos.

Frontier in Space
The Master pretends to sleep on the police ship en route to Draconia.

Planet of the Daleks
Doctor, Jo and Thals grab some kip at the Plain of Stones. Bad move, Vaber is off with the last bombs.

Planet of the Spiders
The Doctor sleeps off his spidery zapping.

Robot
The Doctor sleeps after his regeneration, and after his tussle with the Robot.

The Ark in Space
Sarah goes to sleep rather too well.

Terror of the Zygons
Harry sleeps off his bullet graze in the sickbay.

The Masque of Mandragora
Sarah says the Doctor is thinking, but then he snores. Loudly.

The Androids of Tara
The Doctor snoozes while fishing. Bad move, he wakes to find Farrah's sword setting fire to his hat.

The Leisure Hive
The Doctor grabs a nap on Brighton beach.

Castrovalva
The Doctor and Tegan are seen to sleep, though Nyssa is an early riser.

Kinda
Nyssa, Tegan (and Hindle) sleep. Well, hey – it's a main theme of the story, even if it is a bad move.

Snakedance
*Tegan should have learned from **Kinda**. Very bad move.*

Mawdryn Undead
Turlough sleeps in the sickbay. Bad move, the Black Guardian is in his dreams.

Planet of Fire
Peri sleeps in the TARDIS after Turlough rescues her from drowning, and has nightmares.

Ghost Light
Ace gets a lovely long sleep at Gabriel Chase. Good move.

Doctor Who: The Movie
Grace and Chang Lee both grab some zzzs at the hospital.

PRECOGNITIVE VISION IS IMPOSSIBLE

There have been many psychics and seers in **Doctor Who**, some genuine, some fake. Often it's difficult to predict whether their prophecies will turn out to be correct. The following were proved to be right, or had genuine abilities, often against the odds.

The Doctor
*Premonitions in **The War Machines, The Time Monster, The Deadly Assassin**, and others.*

Cassandra – **The Myth Makers**.

The Seeker – **The Ribos Operation**.

The fortune teller – **Snakedance**.

The Sisterhood of Karn – **The Brain of Morbius**.

Professor Clegg – **Planet of the Spiders**.

Miss Hawthorne – **The Daemons**.

Hieronymous – **The Masque of Mandragora**.

Neeva – **The Face of Evil**.

Leela – **The Robots of Death**.

Li H'Sen Chang – **The Talons of Weng-Chiang**.

Mrs Tyler – **Image of the Fendahl**.

The Mentiads – **The Pirate Planet**v

Organon (by cheating and luck) – **The Creature from the Pit**.

Aukon – **State of Decay**.

Panna and Karuna – **Kinda**.

Elizabeth Rowlinson (a bit) – **Battlefield**

A CLEAR CASE OF MISTAKEN IDENTITY

Occasionally the Doctor is mistaken for someone else – a specific someone rather than a vague representative official. Usually the someone turns out not a good person to be.

- Maximus Petullian – **The Romans**.

- The Abbott of Amboise – **The Massacre of St Bartholomew's Eve**
  Actually, the Abbott is mistaken for the Doctor by Steven, rather than the Doctor being mistaken for him.

- Zeus – **The Myth Makers**.

- Doc Holliday – **The Gunfighters**.

- Salamander – **The Enemy of the World**.

- Sir Reginald Styles – **Day of the Daleks**.

- The Evil One – **Face of Evil**.

- Smutty Thomas's cricketing friend – **Black Orchid**.

- Merlin (or is he really Merlin?) – **Battlefield**.

A TIME LORD GIFT

The Doctor allows his companions to share his knack for understanding and speaking foreign (and alien) languages (or so we learn in **The Masque of Mandragora**). But there have been occasions where characters in **Doctor Who** have slipped into another, untranslated, lingo. We have not included whatever strange language it is that Pigbin Josh spouts in **The Claws of Axos**.

Various Chinese dialects
*Conversations in **The Mind of Evil**, **The Talons of Weng-Chiang**, and quotes from the I-Ching in **Warriors' Gate***.

French
***City of Death**, Polly tries French on the Atlanteans in **The Underwater Menace**, the Doctor tries it on Gulliver in **The Mind Robber**, and Du Pont and Carstairs speak French in **The War Games**. The caption 'PARIS' in **The Reign of Terror** could also be in French.*

Tibetan
*Monks chanting in **The Abominable Snowmen** and the Doctor to K'Anpo **Planet of the Spiders**. The Doctor reads 'Everest in Easy Stages' in **The Creature From the Pit** – but he can't understand it, as it's in Tibetan.*

Arabic
*Namin and the workers in **Pyramids of Mars**.*

High and Low Dutch
*Gulliver tries these on the Doctor in **The Mind Robber**.*

Latin
*Another try by Gulliver in **The Mind Robber** as well as numerous quotes, etcetera, QED.*

Russian
*Russian soldiers in **The Curse of Fenric**, and Petrov says 'good' in Russian in **The War Games**.*

Welsh
*Spoken by the (real) milkman and others in **The Green Death**.*

Aboriginal
*Which Tegan just happens to speak fluently in exactly the right ancient dialect in **Four to Doomsday**.*

Dutch
*Between the youth hostel personnel and others in **Arc of Infinity**.*

Spanish
On Lanzarote in **Planet of Fire**. *Also, spoken by the Dona Arana in* **The Two Doctors**. *Interestingly, when Shockeye the Androgum replies, her response indicates that he is speaking English (though he can later read her cookery books). Polly tries Spanish on the Atlanteans in* **The Underwater Menace**.

German
The War Games *in the 1917 zone. Also, the Doctor pretends to be German in* **The Highlanders**, *and Polly tries German on the Atlanteans in* **The Underwater Menace**.

Gaelic
Jamie's battle cry, and he tries Gaelic on the Atlanteans in **The Underwater Menace**.

Unidentified language spoken by the Doctor
This is tried without success to the Atlanteans in **The Underwater Menace**.

Venusian
Worth an honourable mention. The Doctor chants a Venusian lullaby in **The Daemons, The Curse of Peladon**, *and* **The Monster of Peladon**. *He uses other Venusian vocabulary on occasion ('Thraskin' and 'Plinge' in* **The Time Monster**, *for example), gives useful advice such as 'If the Thraskin puts his fingers in his ears it is polite to shout,' and even tells a joke in* **The Green Death**, *the punchline to which is 'Never trust a Venusian shanghorn with a perigosto stick.'*

HELLO AND GOODBYE

Introductory and valedictory lines of the Doctors are sometimes appropriate and apt. Sometimes less so. This list does not include return visits by Doctors, but is limited to the first and last lines heard on-screen within their own eras.

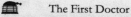

The First Doctor
- First line: 'What are you doing here?'
- Last line: 'Ah yes. Thank you.'

The Second Doctor
- First line: 'Think of one thing... Concentrate on one thing... One thing... It's over. It's over.'
- Last line: 'I refuse to be treated... What are you doing? Stop – you're making me giddy... No – I won't have it. You can't do this to me. No...'

The Third Doctor
- First line: 'Shoes. Must find my shoes... Unhand me, madam.'
- Last line: 'While there's life there's hope.'

The Fourth Doctor
- First line: '... Sontarans perverting the course of human history... I tell you, Brigadier, there's nothing to worry about. The brontosaurus is large and placid. And stupid.'
- Last line: 'It's the end. But the moment has been prepared for.'

The Fifth Doctor
- First line: 'Ah, you've come to help me find the Zero Room. Welcome aboard. I'm the Doctor. Or will be if this regeneration works out. '
- Last line: 'It feels different this time... Adric?'

The Sixth Doctor
- First line: 'You were expecting someone else?'
- Last line: 'Carrot juice, carrot juice, carrot juice.'

The Seventh Doctor
- First line: 'No, no Mel...' [then he wakes up] 'Ahh! That was a nice nap, now, down to business: I'm a bit worried about the temporal

flicker in sector 13... there's the bicentennial refit of the TARDIS to book in, I must just pop over to Centauri 7, then perhaps a quick holiday. Right, that all seems quite clear, just three small points: where am I, who am I – and who are you? The Rani! Stay back!'

- Last line: 'Timing malfunction. The Master – he's out there. I've got to stop him...'

The Eighth Doctor

- First line audience hears (voice-over): 'It was on the planet Skaro that my old enemy the Master was finally put on trial.'
- First line spoken as character (apart from humming): 'Who am I?'
- Last line (so far...): 'Oh no, not again.'

I KNOW WHAT I SAID

More continuity contradictions, but narrative rather than production continuity this time. In a show as long-lasting as **Doctor Who**, it's hardly surprising that a few contradictions and paradoxes arise now and then. Here are some extreme examples to ponder on. We have omitted, for once, the three destructions of Atlantis.

The Daleks are utterly destroyed at the end of their first story. And again (arguably) at the end of **The Evil of the Daleks**. *Yet they keep coming back…*

In **Full Circle** *Romana says the TARDIS weighs 5×10^6 kilos in Alzarian gravity (which seems similar to Earth's). So how did those UNIT soldiers (and others) manage to heave it on to lorries and cart it about so easily?*

The Doctor's age varies dramatically from 450 in **The Tomb of the Cybermen**, *750-ish throughout the third and fourth Doctor's eras, and 900 by the time the sixth Doctor turns up.*

In **The Daleks** *we learn that you have to know exactly how to use the TARDIS key if the lock isn't going to fuse together inside. But through the years loads of people who didn't know this seem to have managed, with the notable exception of the Brigadier in* **Spearhead from Space**.

In **Pyramids of Mars**, *the Doctor tells Sutekh that only he can operate the TARDIS – the controls are isomorphic. He may be kidding, but the fact is repeated by continuity-conscious writers later on in the series history. So how come so many other people, like Steven Taylor for one, can operate the isomorphic controls both before and after this story?*

Yeti balls. In **The Abominable Snowmen** *the Doctor notes that the yeti spheres are empty – they contain just a fraction of the Intelligence's – er – intelligence. But in* **The Web of Fear** *Travers opens up a sphere to tinker with the mechanism inside.*

In **The Dalek Invasion of Earth**, *Dalakanium is a metal. But in* **Day of the Daleks** *it is an explosive.*

In **Warriors of the Deep**, *the Silurians imply that Ichthar at least has met the Doctor before, in* **Doctor Who and the Silurians**. *Unfortunately, there wasn't a Silurian called Ichthar in that story. And they all died anyway. And how come the Silurians and Sea Devils now call themselves Silurians and Sea Devils – one is debunked as inaccurate in* **The Sea Devils**, *the other is a nickname coined by Clark the workman. And the Silurians and Sea Devils didn't know about either name.*

Certainly Gallifreyan patrol stasers and Eldrad's mental weapons don't work in the

TARDIS (**The Invasion of Time** and **The Hand of Fear**). But despite several protestations to the contrary (**The Twin Dilemma**), other people's guns often do (**Earthshock, Attack of the Cybermen**…)

The first time we learn about the Time Lords, and the first time they ever catch up with the Doctor is in **The War Games**. Yet they somehow manage to send the second Doctor off on a mission in **The Two Doctors**. And Victoria gets left behind somewhere, somewhen – despite the fact there was never a chance to fit this story in while she was there, and that the second Doctor was completely unable to control where or when the TARDIS would land. So even if he could get where the Time Lords wanted, he couldn't go back for her.

The Doctor says he has a medical degree in **The Moonbase**, then in **The Krotons** he confesses: 'I'm not a doctor of medicine you know Zoe.'

In **Mawdryn Undead**, the Brigadier is retired and teaching at a school. **Mawdryn** is set partly in 1983 and partly in 1977. Yet the Brigadier is happily sorting out the Loch Ness monster with UNIT in **Terror of the Zygons** which (according to Sarah in Pyramids of Mars) is set in 1980.

Zoe knows what candles are in **The Mind Robber**. But she's forgotten and needs a quick tutorial by the time she gets to **The Space Pirates**.

In **The Daleks' Masterplan**, the Daleks are certain that the Doctor is an alien in a human form. But in **The Evil of the Daleks** they have revised their opinion and think he is 'more than human' merely by virtue of having travelled through time so much.

The Communications Tower on Gallifrey initially has 52 floors in **The Deadly Assassin**. A few scenes later in the same story, they've built on another one!

Time Lords 'live forever barring accidents' in **The War Games**. But in **The Deadly Assassin** we learn they have only twelve regenerations.

The Doctor takes Mel with him at the end of **The Trial of a Time Lord**, after she is brought back from his future. So – they have never actually met.

The Doctor's TARDIS is a Mark One in **Terror of the Autons**. But by **The Deadly Assassin**, it's a Type 40.

A good example of intra-story continuity problems is **Timelash**. The surface of the planet Karfel is shown at the start of the story as being barren rock (and obviously a model). Yet the nearby planet of Bandrill (inhabited by unconvincing puppet people) depends on Karfel for its food. Karfel has cut off food supplies to Bandril, so there is famine there. Yet when the Doctor and Peri examine the vegetation in the citadel on

Karfel, Tekker tells them that all the plants are imported from Bandrill...

Incredible regenerating aliens. Amongst the aliens who undergo amazing transformations between stories with no narrative explanation are the Sontarans (who change height, grow extra fingers, change skin colour...), Silurians (whose third eyes vary from focusing mental energy to flashing when they speak), and Sea Devils (who go gawky and change their tastes in clothes). The Daleks, Cybermen and Yeti changes can be explained away within the narrative, though some changes are difficult to rationalise – like 'advanced' Daleks in **Genesis of the Daleks***, or later Cybermen in sewers and tombs in* **Attack of the Cybermen***.*

NEWS JUST IN

Another sort of continuity error – characters suddenly acquiring information they could not possibly have known. Here are a few examples...

- Zoe knows Slaar's name in **The Seeds of Death** – *clever trick, nobody else ever mentions it.*

- The Doctor mentions in **Image of the Fendahl** *that it was a Fendaleen 'which killed the hiker and Mitchell.' Except he doesn't know about the hiker, and nobody told him Mitchell's name.*

- As mentioned earlier, the Silurians and Sea Devils in **Warriors of the Deep** *know, somehow, that they are called Silurians and Sea Devils. One is an inaccurate guess at a 'home' period, the other coined by the aforementioned workman Clark, driven half-mad by the sight of the string-vested reptiles.*

- The Daleks seem to recognise the Doctor even after he's regenerated – *but, hey, Daleks probably can. Except in* **Day of the Daleks**, *of course.*

- In **Timelash** *Peri suddenly knows all about the Daleks and how they have time tunnels. She can describe the Eye of Orion, and she can recognise Jo Grant from a BBC publicity photo.*

- Also in **Timelash**, *Sezon knows immediately (and with no hints or clues) when Tekker becomes the new Maylin, and when war with Bandril breaks out.*

- Finally, a sort of inverse example. In **Resurrection of the Daleks** *Davros asks Lytton to explain what happened in* **Destiny of the Daleks** *and reacts as if its all news to him.*

I'M SURE SHE'LL TURN UP

STORIES WITHOUT THE TARDIS

Yes, there really have been some! During the third Doctor's era, he sometimes (somehow!) removed the console from the TARDIS – we point out where this happened.

Dalek Cutaway

Doctor Who and the Silurians

The Ambassadors of Death
Console only, removed from TARDIS.

Inferno
Console only, sitting in a garage near the drilling site.

The Mind of Evil
Although there is a scene that may be inside the Master's TARDIS at the end.

The Daemons

Day of the Daleks
Console only.

The Sea Devils

The Sonraran Experiment

Genesis of the Daleks

Remembrance of the Daleks
There is a police box that may be the TARDIS, and Ace stops beside it as if she thinks it is… But you never know – this is 1963 and it might just be a police box.

ANOTHER TARDIS

A list of all the TARDISes that have featured in the programme. It does not list other types of time machine like the one stolen by the Cybermen from Bates, Stratton and others in **Attack of the Cybermen**, or Greel's time cabinet from **The Talons of Weng-Chiang**.

The Doctor's TARDIS
It appears in all stories except those in the list immediately previous.

The Meddling Monk's TARDIS
The Time Meddler, The Daleks' Masterplan.

SIDRATs
*Remote-controlled, limited function TARDIS-technology based machines in **The War Games**. Other Time Lord TARDISes are also in evidence.*

The Master's TARDIS
*Periodically from **Terror of the Autons** to **The Deadly Assassin** (if they are the same TARDIS).*

The Master's other TARDIS
*Periodically from **The Keeper of Traken** onwards.*

Omega's TARDIS
*In **Arc of Infinity**.*

The Rani's TARDIS
*In **The Mark of the Rani** and **Time and the Rani**.*

The Daleks' time machine
*Called a DARDIS in the script, the Daleks have a TARDIS-like time machine in **The Chase** and **The Daleks' Master Plan** (their time technology is different in other stories such as **The Evil of the Daleks**, **Day of the Daleks** and **Resurrection of the Daleks**).*

Drax's TARDIS
*It's somewhere around in **The Armageddon Factor**, but we only see components from it.*

Professor Chronotis' TARDIS
*Disguised as his college rooms in **Shada**.*

IT'S HUGE
DIFFERENT TARDIS ROOMS

Typically when we think of the TARDIS interior, we think of the Console Room. This room is highly variable in geometry during the black and white years, and undergoes numerous re-designs in later years before undergoing a complete refurbishment and expansion for **Doctor Who: The Movie**. But there have been many other rooms within the TARDIS that we have seen throughout the course of **Doctor Who**'s history. We have not listed all the various corridors.

The Console Room
Occasionally with alcove for the Fault Locator, like in **The Daleks**.

Secondary Control Room
From **Masque of Mandragora** *to* **The Robots of Death**.

The Power Room
The Mind Robber *and (looking like an art gallery)* **The Invasion of Time**.

Sleeping Quarters for Barbara, Ian and Susan
In **Inside the Spaceship** *(and similar rooms in* **The Web Planet**).

Food Machine room
Crops up in **The Daleks** *and* **Inside the Spaceship**.

Romana's Room
Crops up in **Full Circle,** *and then in* **Logopolis** *(when it is jettisoned).*

Adric's room
Which becomes Turlough's room in **Terminus**.

Nyssa's room
Seen in **The Visitation, Terminus**, *and others.*

Tegan's room
Seen in **The Visitation, Snakedance,** *and others. This may be the room where Peri is put to bed in* **Planet of Fire**.

The Zero Room
Castrovalva (also jettisoned, along with 25% of the TARDIS' interior)

Cloisters
Seen in **Logopolis** *and* **Doctor Who: The Movie**.

Boot cupboard

Seen in **The Masque of Mandragora**.

Cricket pavilion
Mentioned in **Castrovalva**.

Wardrobe room
Seen in **The Space Museum, The Twin Dilemma, Time and the Rani**.
There's a clothes-rail cupboard in **The Androids of Tara**.

A convenient room
Where Doctor, Peri, Lytton and Griffiths are locked up by the Cybermen in **Attack of the Cybermen**.

Black 'limbo' room
Complete with a fridge used to store segments of the Key to Time in **The Stones of Blood** *and others*.

Sick bay, swimming pool, workshop, conservatory and several other rooms linked by many passages and corridors
All cropping up in **The Invasion of Time**. *It is later mentioned, in* **Paradise Towers**, *that the swimming pool has been jettisoned*.

DON'T TELL ANYONE, BUT...

...It was not perhaps all as much of a mystery as we like to think. Even before they were named, the Doctor's race and planet were mentioned.

100,000 BC
The Doctor mentions his own planet and civilisation, and the concept of the Chameleon Circuit.

Marco Polo
Susan mentions her planet.

The Sensorites
Susan mentions her planet (again).

The Dalek Invasion of Earth
Susan mentions her planet (yet again).

The Time Meddler
The Monk is a member of the Doctor's race, but does not name it or their planet of origin. Or himself, come to that.

The Daleks' Master Plan
The Monk is back, but with no new information.

The Massacre of St. Bartholomew's Eve
The Doctor contemplates going home, but he doesn't say where to.

The Tomb of the Cybermen
The Doctor mentions his family.

The War Games
We finally see the Doctor's home planet, but it is unnamed, unlike the Doctor's race, who are first named by the Alien scientist as the Time Lords.

The Time Warrior
*We have seen that planet twice more (**Colony in Space** and **The Three Doctors**) before the Doctor identifies it to Linx as Gallifrey. Despite the rest of us being in the dark, Linx has heard of Gallifrey and concludes that the Doctor is a Time Lord.*

Planet of the Spiders
The first time regeneration is given an 'official' name.

NOT JUST A TIME LORD

We know very little, really, about the Doctor. What little information we *do* have has been revealed slowly over the years. Here are the stories where we have learned something new and interesting (and note that, despite the considerable hype before -hand, **Silver Nemesis** is not on the list).

📟 **100,000 BC**
Initial information about the Doctor and the TARDIS. We learn that he is an exile, and that Susan is his granddaughter.

📟 **The Time Meddler**
We discover that there are other people from the Doctor's race roaming about the place. The Meddling Monk has a TARDIS the interior of which seems identical to the Doctor's TARDIS.

📟 **The Tenth Planet and The Power of the Daleks**
Our first experience of regeneration.

📟 **The Tomb of the Cybermen**
The Doctor mentions his family to Victoria and tells her he is the equivalent of about 450 Earth years old.

📟 **The War Games**
Enter the all-powerful Time Lords who live forever and have the secret of space/time travel.

📟 **Spearhead from Space**
*The Doctor's first medical that we are privy to – non-human blood, two hearts, low body temperature, facility for self-induced coma... Previously, a chance is missed in **The Dominators** to establish how many hearts the Doctor has. In **Inside the Spaceship** Ian examines the Doctor and notices nothing odd. In **The Sensorites** the Doctor says he's been hit under his heart (singular).*

📟 **Terror of the Autons**
First news about, and appearance of, the Master. His degree in Cosmic Science was higher than the Doctor's.

📟 **The Three Doctors**
We learn about Time Lord hierarchy, the laws of Time, and Omega.

📟 **The Time Warrior**
First time the Doctor's home planet is named – Gallifrey.

Planet of the Spiders
First time regeneration is given a proper term.

Pyramids of Mars
The Doctor's respiratory by-pass system comes in handy when a mummy tries to strangle him.

The Brain of Morbius
News about Morbius and his crusade, and about mindbending contests…

The Deadly Assassin
Most comprehensive information yet on the Time Lords, building on — and contradicting — what we already know. First mention of Rassilon.

The Invisible Enemy
The Doctor mentions that Time Lords can form a neural link and share their brains. He mentions that he lost that particular facility when they 'threw me out.'

The Ribos Operation
Interesting to learn here that the Doctor passed his exams at the Academy by getting 51% at the second attempt.

Shada
Lots of good stuff here about a schism between rival chapters of Time Lords. Pity it was never finished or broadcast.

The Caves of Androzani
The Doctor is apparently allergic to certain gases. His handy stick of celery turns purple if the gases are present. Then, he says, he eats the celery.

The Two Doctors
News of the Rassilon Imprimatur and the symbiotic nuclei Time Lords use to control their TARDISes.

Doctor Who: The Movie
Shock-horror — the Doctor is half human.

TRIVIA

AT YOUR CONVENIENCE
TOILET REFERENCES

Like a number of taboo subjects, **Doctor Who** has tended to skirt around the issue of bodily functions. Ever so infrequently, however, the odd remark has implied a recognition of their existence, such as...

The Robots of Death

All the water on the Sandminer is recycled – to Leela's obvious distaste.

Horror of Fang Rock

Ben is thought to have 'stepped outside for a while' when the Doctor and Leela say they have not seen him on their way in.

The Ribos Operation

On their way somewhere, the Doctor tells K9, 'Don't stop at all the corners.'

The Power of Kroll

The vast amounts of methane being extracted by the refinery are a result of Kroll's digestive processes...

I COULD MURDER A CUP OF TEA

Hot beverages featured in **Doctor Who** is a favourite topic, especially among the more suggestible of us who feel compelled to go and make a cup of something as soon as someone mentions the subject... Ah, that's better. For the sake of comprehensiveness, we have included beverages prepared out of vision, even if there is some doubt as to whether they were ever actually made (we felt sure you would want us to). Also, if a beverage is featured but it is not identified, we have boldly assumed it is tea...

Tea

The Faceless Ones
The Doctor freezes Meadows' cup.

The Evil of the Daleks
Lots of it, too.

The Abominable Snowmen
Tibetan tea with rancid yak butter.

The Web of Fear
Lots of hot, sweet army tea.

The Invasion
Lots of hot, sweet army tea.

The War Games
Lots of hot, sweet army tea.

Spearhead from Space
Lots of... well, guess.

Doctor Who and the Silurians
Er, more of the same really.

The Ambassadors of Death
Liz gives the Doctor a mug of something, which he returns, almost immediately, as if he has drunk it. Probably he's had enough of that hot, sweet army tea by now...

The Mind of Evil
Fu Peng offers the Doctor tea.

The Daemons
Professor Horner drinks what is presumably tea while waiting to go on air. Miss Hawthorne makes tea for herself and Benton in episode four.

The Sea Devils
Hot, sweet navy tea.

The Time Monster

Jo brings the Doctor a cup from which he doesn't drink but tells her he enjoyed it. A cup of tea is transported by TOMTIT in the official demonstration. Tea-leaves taken from another cup are the final ingredient in the Doctor's time-experiment sabotager.

The Three Doctors

Jo serves lashings of stuff in blue plastic mugs — cue the Doctor's silicon-rod gag.

The Green Death

Jo has a cup in episode one, various miners drink tea, and Yates has tea and a biscuit with his guard.

The Time Warrior

When taking in the truth about the situation in medieval England, Sarah says she could murder a cup of tea. Probably none in the country though.

Invasion of the Dinosaurs

The Doctor has his with four sugars.

Image of the Fendahl

With fruit cake!

The Invasion of Time

The Doctor suddenly asks Borusa, 'What's for tea?' by way of demonstrating how to use distracting thoughts.

The Stones of Blood

Vivien Fay has a thermos of (what is probably) tea with her at the stone circle, and Professor Rumford makes cups of (what is probably) tea back at the cottage, to go with Vivien's sausage sandwiches.

The Power of Kroll

The Doctor asks if there will be raspberry jam for tea. Presumably there will be tea for tea too.

Shada

'Milk? One lump or two… Sugar?'

The Awakening

Turlough confesses he's become fond of that brown liquid they have on Earth. 'Ale,' Will Chandler agrees knowingly, but Turlough actually means tea.

Mawdryn Undead

Tea at the Brigadier's hut.

Remembrance of the Daleks

With or without sugar…

Silver Nemesis

Lady Peinforte's house becomes a tea shop.

Coffee

The War Machines

The well-known amnesia cure. 'Coffee?' suggests Sir Charles to cover up the Doctor's outrageous fluff of his lines – 'I wonder, Sir Charles, do you think –' he starts magnificently, before realising it's not his cue at all and finishing lamely: 'No, no. I don't suppose you do.'

The Tenth Planet

Polly puts the kettle on.

The Moonbase

And again. The poison, for a change, is in the sugar.

The Evil of the Daleks

The Doctor and Jamie wait for a clandestine meeting at the 'Tricolour' coffee bar.

The Tomb of the Cybermen

Part of the expedition's packed lunch. Kaftan drugs Victoria's coffee.

Doctor Who and the Silurians

A coffee jug is apparent.

Terror of the Autons

Mrs Farrel is making some coffee in her CSO kitchen when her husband is killed.

The Mind of Evil

The Brigadier's somewhat surreal order is, 'Lay on some coffee, Corporal Bell.'

The Sea Devils

Part of Walker's breakfast.

The Green Death

Mentioned – Cliff tells Jo she can make some coffee; 'Like a dutiful tea girl,' she counters... Some mistake surely?

The Time Warrior

Mentioned but unseen – the Doctor suggests Sarah should make it.

Planet of the Spiders

The smell of Benton's coffee rouses the Doctor from his reverie. Benton, the Doctor claims, makes the finest cup of coffee after Mrs Samuel Pepys.

Image of the Fendahl

Coffee for breakfast at the Priory.

The Trial of a Time Lord (Parts nine to twelve)

'You make a lovely cup of coffee, Janet.'

Cocoa

 The Aztecs

Or at least some sort of Aztec drink made with cocoa beans. Also, Tlotoxl s poisoned brew for Barbara.

 Terror of the Autons

Yates promises to make some for Jo, but on returning to the lab with the stuff, is distracted by having to shoot an animated plastic devil doll.

ANIMAL FIENDS!

Quite a variety of fauna have appeared in the programme over the years, and while this list attempts to be as exhaustive as possible, there may be one of two we have missed – there are obviously things like birds flying in the background of location scenes which we have not included; similarly anything appearing in stock footage we have deemed not to appear in the programme as such (for example, the alligators in **The Dalek Invasion of Earth**). Usually these animals are provided for the production team, occasionally they just turn up all by themselves... We have (most times) excluded visual effects animals, such as the insects and worm in **Planet of Giants**.

- Cats
    - *Planet of the Giants, The Time Monster, (The Green Death – mention of Miss Cartwright's ginger cat), Invasion of the Dinosaurs, Resurrection of the Daleks, The Two Doctors, Survival.*
- Dogs
    - *Doctor Who and the Silurians, The Daemons, The Green Death, Invasion of the Dinosaurs, Robot, The Android Invasion (android ones), The Hand of Fear, Image of the Fendahl, The King's Demons, The Mark of the Rani, Battlefield, Survival.*
- Horses
    - *Marco Polo, The Reign of Terror, The Crusade, The Gunfighters, The Smugglers, The Highlanders, The War Games, The Sea Devils, The Time Monster, The Time Warrior, The Masque of Mandragora, The Deadly Assassin, The Talons of Weng-Chiang, The Androids of Tara, The Visitation, The King's Demons, The Awakening, The Mark of the Rani, Survival.*
- Unicorn
    - *The Mind Robber (played by a horse – no, really).*
- Cows
    - *The Crusade (corpse), The Invasion, The Green Death, Planet of the Spiders, Image of the Fendahl ('Which of you ladies has the time scanner?'), Delta and the Bannermen, Survival (assorted bones from an abattoir).*
- Sheep
    - *The Green Death (of course).*
- Monkeys
    - *Marco Polo.*

Insects

> *The Crusade (ants, flies)*, **The Green Death** *(maggots!)*, **Delta and the Bannermen** *(bees)*, **Ghost Light** *(beetles etc.)*,

Birds

> *The Crusade (hawk)*, **The Ark** *(?)*, **Doctor Who and the Silurians** *(chickens)*, **The Daemons** *(sacrificial chicken)*, **The Three Doctors** *(at the nature reserve)*, **Carnival of Monsters** *(chickens)*, **The Green Death** *(chickens)*, **The Stones of Blood** *(crows)*, **Full Circle** *(pigeons covered in powder paint)*, **The Curse of Fenric** *(doves)*, **Ghost Light** *(stuffed ostrich)*, **Doctor Who: The Movie** *(more chickens)*.

Rats

> *The Reign of Terror (out of vision)*, **The Talons of Weng-Chiang**, **The Visitation**, **Attack of the Cybermen** *(in sewer, but cut from final version)*, **The Two Doctors** *(eaten by Shockeye)*, **Paradise Towers**.

Mice

> *The Daleks' Master Plan.*

Elephants

> *The Ark, Terror of the Autons.*

Lizards

> *The Ark, Silver Nemesis.*

Lions

> *Terror of the Autons.*

Frogs

> *The Claws of Axos.*

Butterflies and Moths

> *The Two Doctors, Ghost Light.*

Snakes

> *Snakedance.*

Spiders

> *Planet of the Spiders, The Deadly Assassin.*

Llamas

> *Silver Nemesis.*

Crocodile

> *The Deadly Assassin (rubber).*

Goats

> *The Daemons (stuffed head)*, **Delta and the Bannermen**.

Fish

> *Doctor Who: The Movie (dead one)*, **The Two Doctors** *(rubber gumblejack…)*

I AM THE DOCTOR AND YOU WILL OBEY ME

Traditionally the province of the Master, the odd bit of hypnosis has been used by the Doctor in his time…

The War Machines (Dodo)
> *To reverse the effects of WOTAN's conditioning, and get information.*

The Abominable Snowmen (Victoria)
> *To get her to remember what happened in the Inner Sanctum.*

The Krotons (Vana)
> *As therapy after her experiences in the Dynatrope.*

The Curse of Peladon, The Monster of Peladon (Aggedor)
> *Not quite hypnosis, but what the Doctor refers to as empathy.*

The Curse of Peladon (Jo Grant)
> *At the same time as Aggedor, but inadvertently.*

The Green Death (Brigadier Lethbridge-Stewart)
> *Inadvertently, while* de-hypnotising *Mike Yates from BOSS's influence.*

Terror of the Zygons, The Hand of Fear (Sarah Jane Smith)
> *In the first case to enable her to survive without oxygen in the decompression chamber, in the second to clear Eldrad's influence from her mind and find out about her/his aims.*

The Invasion of Time (Rodan)
> *To build the D-Mat gun.*

The Ribos Operation (Shrieve)
> *To get past him and gain access to the jewel room.*

Some failed attempts at hypnosis…

The Power of Kroll (Ranquin)
> *The Doctor attempts to hold a conversation with him to get close enough to hypnotise him, but it doesn't work…*

Revelation of the Daleks (Mutant)
> *Almost, but not quite.*

The Trial of a Time Lord (Glitz)
> *Glitz turns out to be more interested in the value of the watch than its hypnotic swinging.*

I TOOK LESSONS FROM JOHN L SULLIVAN HIMSELF

Despite the Doctor's oft-stated assertions that he is never gratuitously violent, most incarnations of the Doctor have shown themselves to be a bit tasty in a fight, to coin a phrase – Troughton, McCoy and McGann being the least prone to violence. The following is a short list of some of those humanoids that have come a cropper at the Doctor's hands. It does not include the countless aliens he has combated.

- **The Reign Of Terror**
  Road Works Overseer
- **The Dalek Invasion of Earth**
  Roboman
- **The Romans**
  Ascaris
- **Kinda**
  Hindle
- **The Visitation**
  Villagers
- **Warriors of the Deep**
  Marine Guard
- **The Power of Kroll**
  Swampie 'fake Kroll'
- **The Keeper of Traken**
  Neman and two fosters
- **The Seeds of Doom**
  Chase's chauffeur and Scorby
- **Day of the Daleks**
  Shura
- **The Time Warrior**
  Guards on gate of Irongron's castle
- **The Green Death**
  Hinks and Global chemicals guards
- **100,000 BC**
  Za (very nearly)
- Various people get the Third Doctor's chest-pinch thing – Stahlman, Leeson etc...

THERE'S BEEN A MURDER

Rarely does the Doctor resort to murder, more usually it's manslaughter, and sometimes it's even justifiable. Decide for yourself in these representative cases, which in the interests of brevity omit aliens (Ice Warriors, Daleks, Cybermen, CyberController, Dominators, Vervoids, etc.).

The War Machines (Professor Krimpton)

> Killed trying to stop the Doctor's reprogrammed war machine from destroying WOTAN. The Doctor didn't do it on purpose, but he might have foreseen something of this sort could happen, and he makes no attempt to save the lives of the people under WOTAN's control.

The Brain of Morbius (Solon)

> Locked in the basement, the Doctor makes a last-ditch attempt to stop Solon perfecting Morbius's new body. He rustles up some cyanide and feeds it up to Solon's laboratory via the ventilation system.

Vengeance on Varos (Guard)

> The Doctor sets the disintegrator gun to go off, and it kills a guard, while helping Jondar escape. The two guards who fall in the acid bath later were an accident, more or less.

The Two Doctors (Shockeye)

> Given a good unhealthy dose of cyanide by the Doctor.

Timelash (The Borad)

> The Doctor deliberately reflects the Borad's death ray back at him using a handy kontron crystal.

The Sea Devils (Sea Devils)

> The Doctor causes the Sea Devils' base to be destroyed by sabotaging the Master's reactivation device. This is ostensibly done to avoid war between the Sea Devils and humans, which seems a tad specious and hypocritical after his condemnation of the Brigadier in **Doctor Who and the Silurians** (although that wasn't much of a condemnation – he didn't resign or anything, did he?).

145

TAKE IT FROM ME, DOCTOR
THINGS STOLEN BY THE DOCTOR

The TARDIS

*Despite assertions in **Doctor Who: The Movie** that the TARDIS is his, on many previous occasions the Doctor has admitted that he 'borrowed' it. He appears to steal it for a second time in **Marco Polo**, when he loses it in a game of backgammon to Kublai Khan. Marco Polo himself returns the TARDIS key and the travellers escape.*

Synestic lock – The Ark in Space

*Pocketed while uncoupling the shuttle craft in the Ark, it later acts as a surrogate cigarette case when it shields the Doctor from Styre's blaster-shot in **The Sontaran Experiment.***

His costume – Spearhead from Space, Doctor Who: The Movie

*In **Spearhead**, the Doctor clothes himself from garments found in the staff rooms of the Ashbridge Cottage Hospital, and this is the costume he appears to keep for the rest of that series. Similarly, the eighth incarnation of the Doctor takes clothing from a hospital staff locker in 1999 San Francisco – specifically a 'Wild Bill Hickok' fancy-dress costume.*

Dr Beavis's car – Spearhead from Space

Escaping from the hospital, the Doctor 'borrows' the vintage car belonging to Dr Beavis, the specialist who has been summoned to investigate his unusual physiology.

Aircar – The Pirate Planet

To get to the Bridge from the city on Zanak, the Doctor lures away the guard of an aircar with a trail of jelly babies, and commandeers it.

A glass – The Power of the Daleks

After managing to imitate the sonic lock of his cell door by using a glass and some water, the Doctor, escaping with Quinn, pockets the glass.

Romana's sonic screwdriver – The Horns of Nimon

Helping to fix the Skonnon spaceship, the Doctor offers to lend Romana his sonic screwdriver, but she has one of her own. The Doctor examines it sceptically, then returns his screwdriver to Romana. However, she notices the switch.

Clothing – The Crusade

Pinched as a disguise by the Doctor and Vicki in Jaffa.

The Master's dematerialisation circuit – Terror of the Autons

Luckily for Earth, this proves incompatible with the Doctor's TARDIS.

The Monk's directional unit – **The Daleks' Master Plan**
> *Luckily for the unpredictable nature of the First Doctor's meanderings,* this *proves to be incompatible with the Doctor's TARDIS.*

The Master's temporal comparator – **Planet of Fire**
> *Perhaps he's just handling goods stolen by Stapley in* **Time-Flight**...

Beryllium Chip – **Doctor Who: The Movie**
> *Stolen from Professor Wagg's clock.*

A CERTAIN FAVOUR

Chaste and family show that it is, there have been quite a few kisses of note over the years.

The Daleks
Ganatus kisses Barbara's hand. In return, she kisses his cheek. Thankfully, they leave it at that.

The Dalek Invasion of Earth
Quick furtive snogs for Susan and David.

The Space Pirates
Madeleine Issigri kisses the Doctor.

The War Games
The Doctor kisses Zoe goodbye in episode one.

The Curse of Peladon
Jo kisses Peladon goodbye.

The Green Death
Jo and Cliff.

The Androids of Tara
Grendel and Lamia, Reynart and Strella.

The Armageddon Factor
The hero and heroine ('Young men are out there dying for it!' he tells her), plus Astra and Merak.

The Keeper of Traken
Tremas and Kassia.

The Two Doctors
Jamie gives Peri a peck, inspired by having earlier seen Anita kiss the Doctor.

The Greatest Show in the Galaxy
Flowerchild and Bellboy.

Doctor Who: The Movie
Doctor and Grace in particular – three times.

JUST PUPPETS, YOU KNOW
REFERENCES TO OTHER TELEVISION SHOWS

There have hardly been any deliberate references to other (real) television programmes in **Doctor Who,** because the show has always striven for a certain freedom from such mundane reality. Much more fun can be had from spotting inadvertent use of programme titles. We have not included references to fictional television programmes such as **The Passing Parade (The Daemons).**

The Aztecs
: *The Doctor's toast to Cameca is 'Happy days'.*

Doctor Who and the Silurians
: *Includes a character called Doctor Quinn.*

Inferno
: *The Doctor asks Greg, when the latter sees him at the TARDIS console, if he expected a rocket with Batman at the controls – of course he could be referring to the comic strip version, but the* **Batman** *TV series was the most public incarnation at that time.*

Colony in Space
: *When the lights go out, Mary Ashe tells Jo that 'Jim'll fix it' – a reference to Jim Holden, the colonists' repairman. (The TV series* **Jim'll Fix It** *did not start until 1975.)*

The Sea Devils
: *The Master watches part of an episode of* **The Clangers** *in his cell, whistling along to it. 'It seems to be some very interesting extraterrestrial life form,' he tells Trenchard. The prison governor does not appreciate the joke: 'Just puppets, you know – for children.'*

The Time Monster
: *Stuart Hyde quips 'Good thinking, Batman' to Ruth Ingram, a reference to the TV show rather than the comic strip.*

The Hand of Fear
: *Doctor Carter describes Sarah's outfit as 'just like Andy Pandy'.*

The Horns of Nimon
: *The Doctor complains that wherever he goes people are pointing phasers at him. He's getting himself confused with someone else, surely.*

Frontios
: *'We must be on the Outer Limits.'*

Delta and the Bannermen

*The Navarino tourists are said to be heading back to 'the rock and roll years', while the Doctor later quotes a line from the theme tune to **Rawhide**.*

Remembrance of the Daleks

*Ace turns on a TV set, and we are led to believe we are about to get the beginning of **Doctor Who**, or its equivalent in the **Doctor Who** universe (of course being November, it's nowhere near 5.15pm because it's broad daylight). Rachel and Alison refer to having worked at the British Rocket Group with 'Bernard' – i.e. **Quatermass**.*

Survival

*There is a **Land of the Giants** annual on a stall at the second-hand shop where Ange is collecting for the hunt saboteurs.*

The Wheel of Fortune

*Nicky Campbell's game show shares its name with episode three of **The Crusade**.*

The Survivors

*Long before Terry Nation's so named his gloomy drama serial, he used it for episode two of **The Daleks**.*

YOU WERE DRUNK
ALCOHOL IN DOCTOR WHO

The Reign of Terror
Wine drinking at the Renan house, and a pub scene in episode six.

The Romans
All that Roman orgying.

The Crusade
Wine.

The Time Meddler
Mead.

The Massacre of St Bartholomew's Eve
Scenes in a tavern in episode one.

The Gunfighters
Charlie the barman kept churning it out. Till Johnny Ringo shot him, anyway.

The War Machines
Not obvious what they're drinking in The Inferno, but there's a pub scene (watching Kenneth Kendal) in episode four.

The Smugglers
Beer drinking.

The Highlanders
Inn scenes.

The Evil of the Daleks
Terrall tries to drink wine but is full of static electricity… Maxtible knocks a bit back too.

The Enemy of the World
Salamander drinks wine. So, unfortunately, does Fedorin.

The War Games
Villar drinks a bit. The Doctor is locked in the château's wine cellar.

Terror of the Autons
Rossini's whisky (as drunk by Tony the strongman).

The Mind of Evil
The Master quaffs wine with his dinner. (The Brigadier says he's bringing in booze for the governor, when he's doing his van-driver act. Actually he's bringing in his troops, of course.)

Colony in Space
Morgan gets drunk and grumpy.

The Daemons
Pub scenes, and the Brig's suggestion of a pint with Yates.

Day of the Daleks
The Doctor's one-man cheese-and-wine society, and whatever wine it is they're drinking on 22nd-century Earth.

The Sea Devils
The Doctor appears to have a whisky and soda in Hart's office in episode four.

The Time Monster
Stuart's plonk (empty bottle only) and the Master's brandy.

Carnival of Monsters
Sundowners, chota pegs etc.

The Green Death
Stevens gives the Brigadier what appears to be whisky, there's wine at the Nuthutch dinner and champagne at the engagement party (the Doctor downs his glass in one go).

The Time Warrior
Sour wine.

The Monster of Peladon
Whatever's in those horn goblets...?

The Android Invasion
People in pub. That said, it's only what the androids are having, so like everything else it's probably not real.

The Brain of Morbius
Château Solon — goes straight to the head...

The Masque of Mandragora
Well, it is Italy.

The Talons of Weng-Chiang
Jago's flask.

The Ribos Operation
Unstoffe's drugged grog for the Shrieve.

The Stones of Blood
De Vries offers sherry.

The Androids of Tara
Mucho vino.

City of Death
The Countess's green chartreuse (or whatever). The Doctor, disappointingly, orders water for everyone at the café ('Make them doubles').

State of Decay
Nice drop of red...

Warriors' Gate
Remember to say 'when'.

The Keeper of Traken
People drinking at Tremas and Kassia's wedding. Tremas is tipsy.

Castrovalva
Castrovalvans drink post-hunt...

The Visitation
Booze found in cellar of house. Adric is wary of it.

Black Orchid
Tegan's screwdriver, and whatever the Cranleighs were having.

Snakedance
Ambril's banquet.

Enlightenment
At the party on Wrack's ship and at dinner with Striker.

The King's Demons
Booze galore at the banquet.

The Awakening
Will likes a drop of ale.

Planet of Fire
'You were drunk,' they tell Timanov of his spiritual experience.

The Mark of the Rani
Tobies are talked of, but we don't see anything being quaffed from them.

The Twin Dilemma
The Doctor remembers getting drunk with Azmael.

The Two Doctors
Barrels of the stuff in Dona Arana's cellar, and the Doctor and Shockeye have several bottles (we are told) in Las Cadenas.

Revelation of the Daleks
Grigory's drink problem (he keeps spilling it).

Battlefield
Shou Yiung's tipple (vodka and Coke), Pat's home brew.

Ghost Light
Drinks at the dinner party.

Survival
Drinks on table outside the Drayton Court pub in Perivale.

Doctor Who: The Movie
Champagne at reception.

NO SMOKE WITHOUT FIRE

TOBACCO IN DOCTOR WHO

100,000 BC

The Doctor smokes a pipe in episode two (Kal's aversion therapy of knocking him over the head is an effective cure, and he never smokes again).

The Reign of Terror

Jules Renan smokes a pipe.

Planet of Giants

Farrow and Forester both smoke cigarettes.

The Gunfighters

Johnny Ringo smokes cigarillos.

The Highlanders

Ffinch smokes a pipe.

The Faceless Ones

Detective Inspector Crossland smokes a pipe.

The Evil of the Daleks

Both Bob Hall and Kennedy smoke cigarettes (Hall rolls his own). Maxtible smokes cigars.

The War Games

Captain Ransome smokes a pipe, as does the Confederate soldier who fires on the ambulance when it first enters the American Civil War zone.

Spearhead from Space

Sam Seeley smokes a pipe.

Terror of the Autons

Rossini is a cigar smoker.

The Mind of Evil

The Master smokes a cigar.

Day of the Daleks

Anat and Monia share a smoke.

The Time Monster

The Master smokes a cigar in Percival's office.

The Green Death

Hinks smokes cigarettes, Stevens smokes cigarettes and a cigar (but not at the same time).

Invasion of the Dinosaurs

A soldier supposedly searching for the Doctor in part five has a crafty smoke.

The Seeds of Doom

Amelia Ducat smokes black cigarette things in a holder.

The Deadly Assassin

*The Doctor sets up a hookah as a diversion (no, this isn't **The Sweeney**). He doesn't actually smoke it, though.*

The Stones of Blood

Among his other unpleasant habits, de Vries is a cigarette smoker.

Enlightenment

One of the sailors has a pipe.

Resurrection of the Daleks

Crew members of the prison ship smoke on the bridge and a soldier has a smoke in the warehouse.

Survival

Cigarettes on sale in Len and Harvey's shop.

RIDICULOUS GARB
THE DOCTOR'S FASHION ACCESSORIES

That is, items of apparel other than the Doctor's standard costume at any given time. We've taken this to mean any items of clothing worn, no matter how briefly. Note also that all the Doctors also wear their predecessor's clothes for a short while, apart from the Second Doctor (whose clothes regenerate with him), and the Eighth Doctor (who regenerates clad only in toe tag and shroud).

First Doctor

Cloak – *100,000 BC, Planet of Giants (with no jacket), The War Machines, The Tenth Planet*.

Fur hat – *100,000 BC, The War Machines, The Tenth Planet*.

Panama hat – *The Daleks, The Chase, The Daleks' Master Plan*.

Scarf – *100,000 BC, The Tenth Planet*.

Cowboy hat – *The Gunfighters (from the TARDIS wardrobe)*.

Atmospheric density jacket – *The Web Planet*
(all right, all right, it's an anorak…)

Crusading clobber – *The Crusade (stolen from Palestinian merchant Ben Daheer)*.

All-over bathing costume – *The Space Museum (mental image only, thank goodness)*.

Second Doctor

Stovepipe hat – *The Power of the Daleks, The Highlanders, The Underwater Menace*.

Cloak – *The Power of the Daleks, The Highlanders, The Tomb of the Cybermen*.

Redcoat uniform – *The Highlanders*.

Washer-woman disguise – *The Highlanders*.

Priestly shawl and headgear – *The Underwater Menace*.

Gypsy disguise (including bandana and dark glasses) – *The Underwater Menace*.

Spacesuit – **The Moonbase** (the TARDIS crew have to get to and from the ship, parked out on the lunar surface).

Fur coat – **The Abominable Snowmen, The Ice Warriors, The Five Doctors**.

Tibetan shawl – **The Abominable Snowmen**.

Salamander disguise – **The Enemy of the World**.

Woolly hat – **Fury from the Deep**.

Life jacket – **Fury from the Deep**.

Alien visor – **The War Games**.

1917 British Army greatcoat and cap – **The War Games**.

Third Doctor

Nightgown – **Spearhead from Space** (in hospital).

Shower cap and towel – **Spearhead from Space**.

Fedora – **Spearhead from Space** (part of Dr Beavis's costume which the Doctor steals, along with his cloak and his car).

Caving gear – **Doctor Who and the Silurians**.

Scientist's short white coat – **Doctor Who and the Silurians** (while working on the plague cure), **The Mind of Evil** (worn with a protective visor while neutralising the Keller Machine).

T-shirt – **Doctor Who and the Silurians** (worn while trying to deactivate the cyclotron).

Spacesuits – **The Ambassadors of Death, Frontier in Space** (based on original **Quatermass** spacesuit).

Dressing gown – **The Ambassadors of Death** (supplied by the space centre).

Asbestos suit – **Inferno** (disguise adopted to infiltrate the drill head area on the alternative Earth).

Submarine escape suit – **The Sea Devils**.

Prison uniform – **Frontier in Space** (kung-fu-style costume for the Doctor's incarceration on the moon).

Spiridon robe – **Planet of the Daleks**.

Miner's overalls and helmet – **The Green Death**.

Milkman's costume – **The Green Death**.

Cleaner's costume – **The Green Death**.

Monk's habit – **The Time Warrior**.

Spider cocoon – **Planet of the Spiders**.

Fourth Doctor

Radiation suit – **Genesis of the Daleks**.

Tam-o'-shanter and tartan scarf – **Terror of the Zygons**.

'Sherlock Holmes' costume – **The Talons of Weng-Chiang** *(this is the only story where Tom Baker's Doctor does not wear a scarf at any point)*.

Painter's smock and beret – **Underworld**.

Lawyer's wig – **The Stones of Blood**.

Waders – **The Power of Kroll**.

Flying-ducks lapel badge – **The Power of Kroll**.

Pallete lapel badge – **City of Death**.

Fifth Doctor

Space helmet(s) – **Four to Doomsday**.

Dressing gown – **Black Orchid**.

Harlequin fancy dress – **Black Orchid**.

Guard's uniform – **Warriors of the Deep**.

Patterned waistcoat – **Planet of Fire**.

Sixth Doctor

Policeman's helmet – **Attack of the Cybermen**.

Miner's coat and muffler – **The Mark of the Rani**.

Necrosian mourning cloak – **Revelation of the Daleks**.

Seventh Doctor

Duffle coat – **The Curse of Fenric**.

Hospital gown – **Doctor Who: The Movie**.

Shroud – **Doctor Who: The Movie** *(once 'deceased')*.

Toe tag – **Doctor Who: The Movie** *(once 'deceased')*.

Eighth Doctor

Shroud – **Doctor Who: The Movie**.

Toe tag – **Doctor Who: The Movie**.

THE DOCTOR'S TREATMENTS
DRUGS AND MEDICINES

There are few instances of narcotics being used in **Doctor Who** for obvious reasons, but there are numerous appearances of medicines, both conventional and fantastical…

Narcotics

- Vraxoin (**Nightmare of Eden**)
  Made from desiccated Mandrel.
- Opium (**The Talons of Weng-Chiang**)
  Mr Sin makes jokes about 'pipe of poppy', and later we see Li H'sen Chang in an opium den, puffing away to dull the pain from his rat-bitten body.
- Chloroform (**The Talons of Weng-Chiang, The Caves of Androzani, Ghost Light**)
  Or some similar substance, used by Greel and Sharaz-Jek to knock Leela and Peri out when kidnapping them, and deftly deployed by Mrs Pritchard.
- Sleeping draughts (**Inside the Spaceship**)
  Administered by the Doctor so he can have peace to try to work out what's wrong with the TARDIS. It proves not to be awfully effective.
- Knockout drugs in drinks (**The Brain of Morbius, The Androids of Tara**)
  Somewhat stronger brews purveyed by more ruthless persons (Solon, Grendel).
- Other knockout drugs (**The Aztecs, The Deadly Assassin**)
  The Doctor unwittingly supplies Ixta with a knockout drug (probably cocaine-based) which is applied to a thorn used to scratch the victim, who turns out to be Ian. The Master uses a drug to feign his own death.

Medicines

- Anti-radiation drugs (**The Daleks, Destiny of the Daleks**)
  *Left outside the TARDIS by the Thals, who later give an extra supply to Susan so that the Daleks will not take them all to analyse. In **Destiny**, the pills are popped by the Doctor and Romana when landing on what turns out to be Skaro. They are later forgotten about, or cease to be crucial to the plot, whichever way you want to look at it.*
- Anti-fungal preparations (**Planet of the Daleks**)
  Both homeopathic remedies, as given by Wester to Jo, and the manufactured version used

by the Thals on the Doctor, are effective in countering the effects of the Fungoid plants on Spiridon.

'Magic' bandage (Inside the Spaceship)

The Doctor hurts his head in the initial explosion, and has a bandage applied to him which contains ointment in coloured bands which gradually disappear as they are absorbed by the wound.

Belladonna antidote (The Sensorites)

The Doctor identifies the mysterious plague which is killing the Sensorites as belladonna poisoning, and knocks up a remedy, saving Ian's life, for one.

Aspirin (The Web Planet)

Barbara gives Vicki aspirin. Vicki thinks they're rather primitive. In **The Mind of Evil***, the Doctor rejects Jo's offer of aspirin, claiming it might kill him. If he'd carried a card to this effect it might have saved some hassle in* **Doctor Who: The Movie***.*

Silurian plague antidote (Doctor Who and the Silurians)

The Young Silurian tries to eradicate humanity by releasing a plague once used by his people to cull mankind's ancestors. Although supposedly incurable, a cure is found for the disease after non-stop toil by the Doctor. Standard broad-spectrum antibiotics were used in the meantime to help slow the disease's progress, and are also used in **The Green Death** *to try to slow up Cliff Jones' infection.*

Anaesthetic (Doctor Who: The Movie)

Part of the Seventh Doctor's fatal treatment.

Unspecified drugs

Given by the Doctor to William de Tornebu after his wounding in **The Crusade***. Bret Vyon cures Steven's blood poisoning in* **The Daleks' Master Plan***. Also, the portreeve's herbal remedy for the Doctor in* **Castrovalva***.*

IT WAS AGONY
INJECTIONS

Related to drugs, a quick run-down of occasions where syringes are used in the series.

- **The Underwater Menace**
- **The Faceless Ones**
- **Doctor Who and the Silurians**
  'It was agony!'
- **The Mind of Evil**
  Preparing people for the Keller Machine.
- **The Sea Devils**
  Clark's tranquilliser
- **The Green Death**
  Cliff's broad-spectrum antibiotics.
- **The Ark in Space**
  Futuristic-style to revive the sleepers, given over the pectoralis major.
- **The Hand of Fear**
  Eldrad gets lanced.
- **The Deadly Assassin**
  Dream sequence one – perhaps the biggest in the series! Also the Master's fake suicide.

Blood samples

A sort of injection in reverse. Blood samples are taken from the infected Winlett in **The Seeds of Doom**. *We also hear of blood being taken from the Doctor in* **Spearhead from Space** *and* **Doctor Who: The Movie**.

THE CATCH-PHRASE IS THE CATCH-PHRASE

Doctor Who is not supposed to be a comedy show, although a number of its writers have been experienced in the field – Terry Nation wrote for the series on the rebound from Tony Hancock. But like many another drama, it too succumbs to the temptation of the catch-phrase. Some of these are associated with the mythology of the show as a whole, some with a particular character or era, others are a writer's whimsy, a way of giving a particular flavour to a story. Notable catch-phrase users are Bob Baker and Dave Martin, but there are other culprits…

'It's bigger on the inside than the outside!'
> *The obvious comment on seeing inside the TARDIS, as the Doctor comments in* **The Three Doctors**, *but among those to use it are Jo in* **Colony in Space**.

'Exterminate!'
> *The Dalek battle cry is synonymous with the whole programme in the public mind. It debuted in their first adventure, and has been with them ever since (the only time it is not used is in their cameo appearance in* **The War Games**, *which is silent).*

'Of course, I should have realised, hmm?'
> *This and its many variations are more or less William Hartnell's main catch phrase, especially the habitual 'hmm's. It is also picked up by Peter Davison's Doctor.*

'When I say run, run!'
> *Originally Patrick Troughton's catch-phrase, appearing in* **The Power of the Daleks** *and* **The Tomb of the Cybermen** *for two. The phrase was resurrected occasionally for later Doctors (Jon Pertwee in* **The Three Doctors**, *for example) and recurs during the 1980s, notably in* **Warriors of the Deep**.

'We will survive.'
> *So insist the Cybermen, especially in* **The Tomb of the Cybermen**.

'Oh my giddy aunt!'
> *Among Troughton's stock are such antiquated phrases as this, uttered at times of extreme peril.*

'Greyhound to Trap One…'
> *UNIT's call signs take some time to settle down, but most frequently use gone-to-the-dogs terminology.*

🏆 'Good grief!'

A phrase much used by both Pertwee's Doctor and the Brigadier, the former when confronted by some unpleasant monstrosity, where it has a hint of scientific curiosity. The Brigadier tends to use it with more of a sense of resigned exasperation.

🏆 'I am the Master and you will obey me!'

Roger Delgado's stock phrase, used when hypnotising people – and you would, too! Eventually resurrected by Anthony Ainley in **Planet of Fire** after a request from a fan who would be upset if we named him.

🏆 'Eldrad must live!'

In **The Hand of Fear** this is what people say when taken over by Eldrad.

🏆 'Contact has been made'

In **The Invisible Enemy** this is what people say when taken over by the Nucleus.

🏆 'Praise the company!'

A standard servile utterance of the subjugated population of Pluto in **The Sunmakers**. The story features much of such linguistic tics, the best example being the anti-catch-phrase of the Gatherer, who uses a different sycophantic word every time he addresses the Collector ('your excellency', 'your immensity' etc).

🏆 'The Quest is the Quest!'

The Minyans' motto in **Underworld**.

🏆 'Weakling scum!'

The Co-pilot's dismissive opinion of the Anethan sacrifices in **The Horns of Nimon**. A classic crap science fiction line.

🏆 'The Wasting is . . . the Wasting!'

Unfortunately, while just about everyone tells us this in **State of Decay**, we never actually discover what the Wasting really is.

🏆 'Excellent!'

Cyber-catch-phrase, associated with **Earthshock** and subsequent Cyber-stories, where it is usually uttered by David Banks as the various Cyberleaders.

🏆 'Brave heart, Tegan!'

A Davison catch-phrase, used in **Earthshock** for one, **Warriors of the Deep** for another, and one of Tegan's last lines in **Resurrection of the Daleks**.

🏆 'Build high for happiness!', 'Cowardly cutlets!', 'Ice hot!' etc

In **Paradise Towers** the Kang street gangs had their own particular mangled *vocabulary, characterised by these and similar catch phrases. Similarly, the Caretakers couched all their utterances in quotes from their rule book, all 'paragraph' this, 'subsection' that.*

'Ace!'

*Customary saying of the character of the same name, hence the name... One of numerous examples of 1980s street lingo perpetrated by Sophie Aldred's character, the other most prevalent being her reference to the Doctor as 'Professor', despite his forbidding her to do so at the end of her first adventure, **Dragonfire**.*

'I'm glad you're happy!' . . . 'I'm happy you're glad!'

***The Happiness Patrol** is another story featuring endemic jargon, a set phraseology helping to define, in this case, the oppressive and clichéd regime on Terra Alpha.*

'Wicked!'

*Ace's phrase, which gets passed on to the Pipe People in **The Happiness Patrol**.*

'RABBITS!'
SWEARING

Well, obviously no one really swears, at least not obviously, on screen, in **Doctor Who**. However, the various novels published over the years have come up with a few instances, beginning with the use of 'bastard' in Ian Marter's novelisation of **The Enemy of the World** in 1981. Instead of such unacceptable oaths, from time to time television writers have employed a variety of near-equivalents, either the milder standard rude words or assorted euphemisms. There is also a stratum of lines which don't quite come out as they appear to have been intended, and sound suspiciously coarse...

'Rabbits!'

Almost a catch-phrase of Tegan's.

'Spack off!'

*Whatever it was that Tom Baker was supposed to say to the Daleks in **Destiny of the Daleks**, it comes out like this.*

'Sod off!'

*This could either be a mishearing or a mispronunciation of a line of William Hartnell's, spoken to a guard in **The Romans**.*

'Will you please stop buggering me?'

*Again, one has to presume that it is Hartnell's pronunciation and that he actually asks Steven to stop bothering him in **The Time Meddler**.*

'Blast!'

*Romana's repeated exasperation at being unable to fix K9 in **Meglos**.*

'Balled up!'

*Captain Hopper's colourful description of the state of repair of his ship after Toberman has indulged in a little sabotage, in **The Tomb of the Cybermen**.*

'Tail.'

*Irongron's description of what part of Sarah his guards will grab in recapturing her in **The Time Warrior** – much too rude to explain...*

'Shit!'

*So one of the fugitives at the start of **Timelash** curses, not quite under his breath, when they are being chased. No, really.*

'Only children believe that crap!'

*Grace brings **Doctor Who** firmly into the 90s with an utterance that would have had most adults in 1963 running behind the sofa.*

ATTACK OF THE SEAWEED MONSTER WHICH CAN BE DESTROYED BY SOUND
STORY TITLES WHICH GIVE THE GAME AWAY

Here are a few of the occasions when despite trying to preserve an air of mystery about what's going on, or who is behind the Sandminer murders, or what Solon is up to, or why everyone in Devesham is behaving so oddly, the production team have made one small slip.

- Planet of Giants
- *Anything* of the Daleks
- The Three Doctors (etc.)
- The Sontaran Experiment
- The Android Invasion
- The Brain of Morbius
- The Robots of Death
- Attack of the Cybermen

TITLES OF DOOM
LEAST APPROPRIATE STORY TITLES

Doctor Who and the Silurians

He isn't called Doctor Who, and they aren't actually Silurians. Otherwise fine.

Revenge of the Cybermen

An indication of the main problem with this story – Cybermen should not be emotional and certainly have no thoughts of revenge. Ahem.

Planet of Evil

Actually, it isn't. It's saving the universe.

The Deadly Assassin

What assassin isn't?

The Invisible Enemy

Which isn't invisible, just small.

City of Death

Well, it's mainly set in a city and only a few people die.

Nightmare of Eden

Actually quite appropriate, but for all the wrong reasons.

Four to Doomsday

Four what, exactly? Days till the ship arrives? Races of people? Visits by Monarch to Earth? Episodes? Maybe it's over-appropriate...

Resurrection of the Daleks

Er, actually it's Davros who is woken up.

The Twin Dilemma

Just silly.

Revelation of the Daleks

What revelation?

Remembrance of the Daleks

What memory?

State of Decay

*A throwaway line which must have sounded better than **The Wasting**, the story's original title.*

The Enemy Within

*If this really were the title of **Doctor Who: The Movie**, we'd include it. Within what, pray?*

Most inappropriate titles for individual episodes

The End of Tomorrow
Episode four of **The Dalek Invasion of Earth**. *And it's got us stumped.*

The Waking Ally
No relationship at all to the events of episode five of **The Dalek Invasion of Earth**.

The Death of Time
Again, nothing remotely related to episode two of **The Chase**.

DOCTOR WHO?

The **Doctor Who** gag has been used on many occasions. And each time it's as if we won't have heard it before. Here are the times that the Doctor is credited with this name, either as a joke or because someone somewhere thought it *was* actually his name.

100,000 BC
> *The Doctor started it himself, of course.*

The Death of Doctor Who
> *The title of episode five of* **The Chase***. (Actually, he doesn't die.)*

The Gunfighters
> *'Your humble servant, Doctor Caligari,' the Doctor introduces himself to Bat Masterson. I suppose we can forgive him for asking incredulously, if predictably, 'Doctor Who?'*

The War Machines
> *'Doctor Who is required,' by WOTAN. Obviously nobody programmed the computer to ignore the end credits.*

The Highlanders
> *The Doctor's alias Doktor von Wer is the German for Doctor Who.*

The Underwater Menace
> *The Doctor signs his note to Zaroff 'Doctor W.'*

Doctor Who and the Silurians
> *The title of the story. Eh, what?*

The Curse of Peladon
> *The Earth delegate, Amazonia, turns up in the last moments seemingly just to ask, 'What Doctor, Doctor Who?'*

The Mutants
> *The Investigator cracks the old 'Doctor Who?' joke yet again.*

Black Orchid
> *'Doctor Who?' Lady Cranleigh asks coyly, with a knowing look in her eye.*

Bessie
> *The Doctor's car number is WHO 1 (except in long shots where it's WVO 2M, and* **Battlefield** *where it's WHO 7) for no very good reason. Just a quirk of the DVLC, one supposes.*

GOING FOR A SONG

It's not often that the Doctor breaks into song. But here are a few instances.

The Chase

'What's that awful noise?' asks Barbara. Perhaps he was inspired by the Beatles earlier in the episode.

Spearhead from Space

The Doctor sings word- and tunelessly in the shower.

Doctor Who and the Silurians

The Doctor knows a tune for Lewis Carroll's poem, 'Jabberwocky'.

Inferno

The Doctor sings 'La dona e mobile' as he motors along in Bessie.

Terror of the Autons

'I don't want to set the world on fire,' as he starts on his solid-state micro-welding, as pioneered by the Lamadeens (who have nine opposable digits).

The Curse of Peladon, The Monster of Peladon

Venusian lullaby sung to the tune of 'God Rest You, Merry Gentlemen' to appease Aggedor.

Death to the Daleks

The Doctor sings 'I Do Like to be Beside the Seaside' as he and Sarah prepare for their holiday on Florana.

Robot

Skipping song, 'Mother, mother, I feel sick. Send for the doctor quick-quick-quick...'

The Talons of Weng-Chiang, The Invasion of Time

The Doctor whistles 'Colonel Bogie'.

Black Orchid

'I Want to be Happy,' the Doctor croons as he runs his bath.

The Five Doctors

'Who unto Rassilon's tower would go...' chants the Second Doctor. 'Are you in pain?' the Brigadier asks with his usual tact.

The Two Doctors

The Sixth Doctor hums tunes from The Barber of Seville.

The Happiness Patrol

A quick burst of 'As Time Goes By'.

AIDW
ACRONYMS IN DOCTOR WHO

There have been many acronyms used over the years on **Doctor Who**. Putting aside the strange coincidence that even the alien ones translate into our own alphabet, here's a selection (omitting those in common Earth usage, including RHIP – Rank Has Its Privileges – cited by Yates in **Day of the Daleks**).

TARDIS

>*Time and Relative Dimension In Space (**100,000 BC** and onwards. More usually, the D stands for Dimensions).*

IDBI

>*I Don't Believe It (Steven's response to the above in **The Time Meddler**).*

UGH

>*United Galactic Headquarters (**Dalek Cutaway**, and by implication **The Daleks' Master Plan**).*

SSS

>*Space Special Security (**Dalek Cutaway**, **The Daleks' Master Plan**).*

WOTAN

>*Will Operating Thought ANalogue (**The War Machines**).*

ISC

>*International Space Command (**The Tenth Planet**).*

CT

>*Chameleon Tours (**The Faceless Ones**).*

IE

>*International Electromatics (**The Invasion**).*

UNIT

>*United Nations Intelligence Taskforce (**The Invasion** and onwards).*

HADS

>*Hostile Action Displacement System (**The Krotons**).*

SIDRAT

>*Not explained in the programme, but it's TARDIS backwards (**The War Games**).*

IMC

>*Interplanetary Mining Corporation (**Colony in Space**) (or Issigri Mining Company in **The Space Pirates**).*

TOMTIT
*Transmission Of Matter Through Interstitial Time (**The Time Monster**).*

BOSS
*Bimorphic Operational Systems Supervisor (**The Green Death**).*

MSC
*Marine Space Corps (**Death to the Daleks**).*

IRIS
*Image Reproduction Integrating System (**Planet of the Spiders**).*

SRS
*Scientific Reform Society (**Robot**).*

K1
*Kettlewell 1 (**Robot**).*

CIA
*Celestial Intervention Agency (**The Deadly Assassin**).*

DE
*(Bio-)Data Extract (**The Deadly Assassin**).*

SSSS
*Sontaran Special Space Service (**The Invasion of Time**).*

C19
*Not explained, but possibly the government department in charge of UNIT (**Time-Flight**).*

WHY, THAT'S AN ANAGRAM OF... HOW INTERESTING

Among the sources of inspiration that writers draw on for the names of their monsters and alien races, the anagram is one. When he was asked where he came up with the name Dalek, Terry Nation said he got it from a volume of an encyclopaedia which covered DAL to LEK. He later admitted he made this up. This has not deterred some **Doctor Who** experts from rearranging their volumes of the London telephone directory so it can be read DALEK. However, for those of you outside London (where the phone books no longer work like that anyway), here are some other examples:

Kaled

Anagram of Dalek, *the life form into which Davros mutates the Kaleds in* **Genesis of the Daleks**.

Dalek

Anagram of Kaled, *the life form into which Davros mutates the Kaleds. But you guessed that from the previous one, didn't you?*

Drashig

A coincidence, of course, but this ferocious creature from **Carnival of Monsters** *is an anagram of* dishrag.

Foamasi

The alien racketeers in **The Leisure Hive** *are an appropriate anagram of* Mafiosa.

Sir Giles Estram

No prizes for guessing that Sir Giles, in **The King's Demons**, *is really the* Master.

Androgums

The gourmands *of* **The Two Doctors**.

HIT AND MYTH
FAN MYTHS

Over the years, some fans of the programme have exhibited a gullibility equalled only by the ability of others to create hoaxes. Whether by accident or, more rarely, design, here are some of the 'facts' that have passed into fan mythology.

The first episode of **Doctor Who** was transmitted at 5.25
> *It is commonly believed that the first episode was transmitted ten minutes late because of delays following President Kennedy's assassination the previous day. In fact, **An Unearthly Child**, the very first episode, went out at 5.16:30, only 90 seconds later than scheduled.*

Doctor Who was transmitted live
> *This never happened, though transmission was often a very few weeks after recording. But couple the live transmission myth with Jacqueline Hill's claim that 'It was the Daleks that made the programme' and you get a charmingly bizarre image.*

Polly Lopez
> *It is common belief that Polly's surname was Lopez. The only possible reason for this is that the alien who replaces her in **The Faceless Ones** has a passport in the name of Michelle Leupi. The **Doctor Who** production office intended Polly's surname to be Wright, but it is never used in the programme.*

'Reverse the polarity of the neutron flow.'
> *This was not actually a very common line of the Third Doctor's. In fact, it is only used in anything close to this form during his era in **The Sea Devils**.*

The Tribe of Gum
> *This was never intended to be the title of the first story, despite what many people think. It was slated as **100,000 BC** though the overall story titles were never shown on screen in those days. Similarly, the second story was actually **The Mutants** and not, as usually referred to, **The Daleks**. Strangely, those same pedants who insist that we get the name of the first story 'correct' are not at all concerned about calling the second story by its real name – that would be confusing!*

Troughton in colour
> *There still persists, despite all the evidence to the contrary, a theory that some Patrick Troughton stories – in particular the studio film sequences for the final episode of **The Evil of the Daleks** – were made in colour. The theory goes that this was a test prior to the BBC's start of colour transmission, which started in limited form in July 1967 (tests having been conducted continuously since the 1950s).*

♟ Female Doctor

> *There have never been any serious plans to cast a woman in the role of the Doctor, whatever the press might have us think. Tom Baker was the first to throw this out as a (humorous) possibility.*

♟ Terry Nation

> *Even Trivial Pursuit insists that Terry Nation, creator of the Daleks, also invented* **Doctor Who**. *But he didn't.*

♟ **The Daleks of Skaro**

> *Now the truth can be told. It is documented fact that Terry Nation tried to launch a Dalek television series in the USA in the late 1960s. Nothing ever came of it, but this did not upset some eager fans in the late 1980s who, undeterred, provided a script for the second episode. Hawked round the fan community, it gained a lot of credibility, including an article in a major magazine – sadly pulled at the last moment when the truth dawned. The script contained numerous in-jokes, dialogue from bona fide Dalek stories lifted verbatim, and humorous character names (the security guards were John, Scott and Martin). The titles of every Terry Nation-scripted* **Doctor Who** *story and episode, as well as every* **Blake's Seven** *episode title, were included in stage directions and dialogue. Yet still some fans think the script is genuine. In fact, we can reveal exclusively, it was written by Peter Anghelides, Craig Hinton, Andy Lane, Andrew Martin and Justin Richards.*

YOU'RE TREATING US LIKE CHILDREN

Many children and babies have appeared in **Doctor Who**. We have made an arbitrary distinction between children and young adults, and we have generally excluded people in the background in location filming. Also, we have not generally included companions, although Vicki and Zoe in particular were very young and Cranleigh does refer to Nyssa and Adric as 'children' in **Black Orchid**. Susan appears to be a child, though she doesn't use this as an excuse not to marry in **The Aztecs** or **The Dalek Invasion of Earth**. Anyway, since she is a Time Lord, she is probably considerably older than you are. Children appearing as characters other than children (for example, Quarks in **The Dominators**) are also omitted.

- Schoolchildren and cave-kids – **100,000 BC**.

- Jean-Pierre – **The Reign of Terror**.

- Children in the market and child slaves – **The Romans**.

- Baby carried by mother as she leaps overboard from the *Mary Celeste* – **The Chase**.

- Boy and girl in Agamemnon's tent – **The Myth Makers**.

- Child Guardians – **The Ark**.

- Children – **The Savages**.

- Child priests – **The Underwater Menace**.

- Children in the Land of Fiction – **The Mind Robber**.

- Axon boy and girl (well, sort of) – **The Claws of Axos**.

- Neophite and Baby Benton – **The Time Monster**.

- Village children – **The Daemons**.

- Child slaves – **The Day of the Daleks**.

- Xoanon's child-voice calls out 'Who am I?' – **The Face of Evil**.

- Child Trogs – **Underworld**.

- Baby Pangol – **The Leisure Hive**.

- The Marshchild and the Outlers – **Full Circle**.

Kassia is a child in a flashback sequence – **The Keeper of Traken**.

Children playing, in particular the girl who helps the Doctor count to three – **Castrovalva**.

Kinda children – **Kinda**.

Children at barrel organ – **Arc of Infinity**.

Children at puppet show (*Punch and Snakey?*) – **Snakedance**.

Schoolboys; Tegan and Nyssa regressed to children – **Mawdryn Undead**.

Will Chandler – **The Awakening**.

Handbag-snatching youth – **The Awakening**.

The Bangerter children on Lanzarote – **Planet of Fire**.

Romulus and Remus – **The Twin Dilemma**.

Village children – one kicked over by Jack Ward, one paid by the Rani to advertise her bath house, also Josh's baby – **The Mark of the Rani**.

Tribe children – **The Trial of a Time Lord** (parts one to four).

Kangs – **Paradise Towers**.

The Chimeron Princess (and other children) – **Delta and the Bannermen**.

Stellar – **Dragonfire**.

Schoolchildren, especially the girl linked to the Dalek battle computer – **Remembrance of the Daleks**.

The Whizz Kid – **The Greatest Show in the Galaxy**.

Baby Audrey (Ace's mother), Jean and Phyllis – **The Curse of Fenric**.

Squeak and others – **Survival**.

TIME AND RELATIVES

A list of all the characters who are related to other characters in **Doctor Who** would take a whole book of its own. But, undeterred, here's a good crack at some of the more important associations. These are blood relationships only, so marriages are not included, though some can be deduced – it doesn't take a genius to work out that Ivo and Martha are husband and wife, for example. Equally, the list does not include Peri and her stepfather (Howard Foster, **Planet of Fire**). We never see her mother. The Doctor mentions his relatives in **The Tomb of the Cybermen**, but despite suggestions that he may be related to Borusa and/or the Master, there is no 'proof' of these claims. **K-9 and Company** is excluded, partly as it isn't true **Doctor Who** and partly because everyone in that seems to be related to everyone else.

- The Doctor and Susan – grandfather and granddaughter (**100,000 BC** to **The Dalek Invasion of Earth** and **The Five Doctors**).

- Auntie Vanessa and Tegan – aunt and niece (**Logopolis**).

- Andrew Verney and Tegan – grandfather and granddaughter (**The Awakening**).

- Colin Frazer and Tegan – cousins (**Arc of Infinity**).

- Bret Vyon and Sarah Kingdom – brother and sister (**The Daleks' Master Plan**).

- Adric and Varsh – brothers (**Full Circle**).

- Ivo, Martha and Karl – father, mother and son (**State of Decay**).

- King Peladon of Peladon and Queen Thalira of Peladon – Father and daughter (**The Curse of Peladon, The Monster of Peladon**).

- The old Duke and Giuliano – father and son (**The Masque of Mandragora**).

- Count Federico and Giuliano – uncle and nephew (**The Masque of Mandragora**).

- Professor Travers and Anne Travers – father and daughter (**The Web of Fear**).

Professor Watkins and Isobel Watkins – uncle and niece (**The Invasion**).

Antodus and Ganatus – brothers (**The Daleks**).

Draconian Emperor and Draconian Prince – father and son (**Frontier in Space**).

Ace and Audrey Dudman – daughter and mother (**The Curse of Fenric**).

Ace and Kathleen Dudman – granddaughter and grandmother (**The Curse of Fenric**).

Mena and Pangol – mother and son (**The Leisure Hive**).

Professor Watson talks to one of his children and his wife on the phone when he thinks he's about to die as the reactor goes critical (**The Hand of Fear**).

Romulus and Remus and Professor Sylvest – twin brothers and their father; mother is mentioned (**The Twin Dilemma**).

Horg and Hur – father and daughter (**100,000 BC**).

Maylin Rennis and Vena – father and daughter (**Timelash**).

Victoria and Edward Waterfield – daughter and father (**The Evil of the Daleks**).

Theodore Maxtible and Ruth Maxtible (who is engaged to Arthur Terrall) – father and daughter (**The Evil of the Daleks**).

Jules Renan and Danielle – brother and sister (**The Reign of Terror**).

Anne Chaplet and Dodo Chaplet – possible descendent (**The Massacre of St Bartholomew's Eve**).

General Cutler and Terry Cutler – father and son (**The Tenth Planet**).

Arbitan and Sabetha – father and daughter (**The Keys of Marinus**).

Balaton, Pralix and Mula (who is engaged to Kimus) – father, son and daughter (**The Pirate Planet**).

Selris and Thara – father and son (**The Krotons**).

Senex and Cully – father and son (**The Dominators**).

Dom and Madeleine Issigri – father and daughter (**The Space Pirates**).

Major Daly and Clare Daly – father and daughter (**Carnival of Monsters**).

Mrs Smith and Mike – mother and son (**Remembrance of the Daleks**).

Sabor, Neska and Arak, Tuar, Rega – father and mother of the two brothers and their sister (**Planet of the Spiders**).

Marcus and Lawrence Scarman – brothers (**Pyramids of Mars**).

Arthur Stengos and Natasha – father and daughter (**Revelation of the Daleks**).

Martha Tyler and Jack Tyler – mother and son (**Image of the Fendahl**).

King Richard and Joanna – brother and sister (**The Crusade**).

Ibrahim and the bandit – brothers (**The Crusade**).

Saladin and Saphadin – brothers (**The Crusade**).

Haroun, Maimuna and Safiya – father and daughters (**The Crusade**).

Nyssa and Tremas – daughter and father (**The Keeper of Traken**).

Aris and the Kinda man played by Mike Mungarvin (who according to popular myth is called Ilbow since their mother could not tell them apart) – brothers (**Kinda**).

Squire John, Charles and Elizabeth – father, son and daughter (**The Visitation**).

Lady Cranleigh, Lord Cranleigh, George Cranleigh – mother and sons (**Black Orchid**).

Tanha and Lon – mother and son (**Snakedance**).

Mr Farrel, Mrs Farrel and Rex – father, mother and son (**Terror of the Autons**).

Captain Revere and Plantagenet – father and son (**Frontios**).

Beyus, Faroon and Sarn – father, mother and daughter (**Time and the Rani**).

Delta and the Chimeron Princess – mother and daughter (**Delta and the Bannermen**).

Mrs Pritchard and Gwendoline – mother and daughter (**Ghost Light**).

Customer on Iceworld and Stellar – mother and daughter (**Dragonfire**).

Midge and Squeak – brother and sister (**Survival**).

SICK MINDS AND BODIES

Viruses and diseases have loomed large in the history of **Doctor Who**. This list discounts diseases that aren't really diseases at all, like the deadly nightshade poisoning the Sensorites suffer (**The Sensorites**), the mutation of the Solonians (**The Mutants**), and the effects of Stahlman's gas and the associated green liquid (**Inferno**).

Spectrox Toxaemia
> *Which can be cured by the milk of a queen bat* (**The Caves of Androzani**).

Infection from waste products of Global Chemicals
> *Which enlarges insects but makes humans bright green and kills them* (**The Green Death**).

Movellan Virus
> *Used to defeat the Daleks* (**Resurrection of the Daleks**).

Germ warfare, plague missiles and bacteria bombs
> *Used by the Daleks* (**The Dalek Invasion of Earth, Planet of the Daleks, Death to the Daleks, Resurrection of the Daleks**).

Dodo's cold
> *Which severely affects the humans with reduced immunity* (**The Ark**).

The Virus swarm
> *The Nucleus of which infects the Doctor's mind/brain interface* (**The Invisible Enemy**).

Kraal virus
> *Intended to destroy humanity, but accidentally kills Styggron* (**The Android Invasion**).

Neurotrope X
> *Plague used by the Cybermen to attack humans. Characterised by black or inflamed lines on skin* (**The Moonbase, Revenge of the Cybermen**).

Great Space Plague
> *Referred to in several stories. They may or may not refer to the same plague, which may or may not have been a Dalek bacterial attack* (**Carnival of Monsters, Frontier in Space, Death to the Daleks**).

Varga infection
*Causing humans to mutate into Varga plants if they are stung by one (**Dalek Cutaway, The Daleks' Master Plan**).*

Lightwave sickness
*Affects some of the Daleks who are using an anti-reflecting light wave to become invisible (**Planet of the Daleks**).*

Fungoids
*Juice from these plants is squirted at a target. If it is not treated, victims break out in a fungal infection which eventually engulfs them (**Planet of the Daleks**).*

Bubonic plague
*The Black Death, a strain of it enhanced by the Terileptils, or a cover story for the Silurian plague (**The Visitation, Doctor Who and the Silurians**).*

The Silurian plague
*Disseminated via an infected Major Baker to destroy mankind (**Doctor Who and the Silurians**).*

Taran plague
*Wiped out a large proportion of the population of Tara. This was when they started replacing the populace with androids (**The Androids of Tara**).*

Chemical and germ warfare
*Created the Mutos. Davros's experimentation determined the ultimate end of the mutational cycle, and he genetically engineered the end result to create the Dalek – an 'improvement' on the creature the Kaled race would eventually evolve into (**Genesis of the Daleks**).*

Metal virus
*Developed by Professor Kettlewell to attack and break down the living metal he invented. There's a bit of luck (**Robot**).*

Antimatter infection
*Mutates Professor Sorenson into Anti-Man (**Planet of Evil**).*

Krynoid plant infection
*Winlett and Keeler both suffer the indignity of having their blood change to what the Doctor describes as 'vegetable soup', and then turn into Krynoids (**The Seeds of Doom**).*

Radiation sickness
*Or the threat of it (**The Daleks, The Android Invasion, The Hand of Fear, Destiny of the Daleks, Terminus**).*

Distronic Toxaemia
*Affects the slave workers loading distronic explosives into a missile for the Thals (**Genesis of the Daleks**).*

Lazars' disease
*Which has some similarities to, but is definitely not, leprosy (**Terminus**).*

Wirrn infection
*Actually closer to having eggs laid inside your body. Alien before the film was made (**The Ark in Space**).*

Alzarian infection at Mistfall
*Not clear how much is natural evolution from Eggs to Marsh Spider to Marsh Man to Terrodanian nouveau. But Romana is infected when bitten by a spider (**Full Circle**).*

WHEREVER I HANG MY HAT

Over the years, fixtures and fittings have come and gone from the TARDIS console room. It would be a mammoth, and probably impossible, task to document everything that has ever been there (especially in **Doctor Who: The Movie**), so instead, here are just a few of the more notable or absurd.

- Lectern
  *An original piece, also pops up in **The Time Monster** and, in 'regenerated form', in **The Pirate Planet**.*

- Ormulu clock
  *Another original. Notable for its melting face in **Inside the Spaceship**.*

- Hatstand
  *Various stories from the Fourth Doctor's time onwards (for example, **The Invasion of Time** and a strange version in **Image of the Fendahl**), notably all of the Peter Davison era and especially **Frontios**.*

- Table
  *Lots, especially for chess in **The Sun Makers**, **Enlightenment**, etc.*

- Silver drum
  *Arrives in the TARDIS in **Colony in Space**. Strangely enough, it also appears in the Primitive city…*

- Emergency oxygen supply
  Planet of the Daleks.

- Roll-out bed and accompanying wardrobes
  Planet of the Daleks.

- Cupboard full of junk, including fishing rod
  The Androids of Tara.

- Big chest
  ***The Power of the Daleks** (containing clothes), **The Abominable Snowmen** (containing clothes and holy ghanta), **The Wheel in Space** (containing Zoe), and others.*

- Chair
  *For Barbara to collapse in on take-off in **100,000 BC**, with forcefield built in for **The Daleks' Master Plan**, and for Jamie and the Doctor to sleep in (at different times) in **The Mind Robber**, plus others.*

Glass-topped table
Handy place to keep your Key To Time in **The Armageddon Factor**.

Library steps
Logopolis.

Police box
Logopolis.

Wicker stools
Which Tegan and Nyssa just carry in and then sit on for no very good reason in **Mawdryn Undead**. *Similar furniture is featured in* **The Five Doctors**.

JUST ONCE I'D LIKE TO MEET AN ALIEN MENACE THAT WASN'T IMPERVIOUS TO BULLETS

It became a cliché that UNIT blazed away to no effect at the invading monsters. But actually, relatively few races are truly impervious.

Daleks
> *Generally they can resist bullets but their eyepieces are shot off in various stories including **Resurrection of the Daleks** and **Revelation of the Daleks**. (Orcini destroys a Dalek using bullets with bastic heads.)*

Cybermen
> *Usually they're fine with bullets. But in **The Invasion** bazookas and grenades have an effect, while by **Attack of the Cybermen** they are extremely delicate, and not at all impervious to Griffiths' or Russell's handguns.*

The Destroyer
> *He's killed by silver bullets but immune to others in **Battlefield**.*

Autons and other Nestenes
> *They're thoroughly immune in **Spearhead from Space** and **Terror of the Autons**.*

The alien ambassadors
> *They ignore bullets in **The Ambassadors of Death**.*

Yeti
> *Bullets can't hurt them in **The Abominable Snowmen** and **The Web of Fear**.*

Bok
> *Blown up by a bazooka, he swiftly reforms. Otherwise unfazed in **The Daemons**.*

Azal
> *No chance (**The Daemons**).*

Gell Guards
> *They just keep on coming through the gunfire in **The Three Doctors**.*

Eldrad
> *Being silicon-based in **The Hand of Fear**, (s)he's fine against bullets. Presumably the Ogri in **The Stones of Blood** are also therefore similarly bullet-proof.*

Ice Warriors
*As demonstrated in **The Seeds of Death**.*

Osiran Service Robots
*The mummies suffer various shotgun blasts without much discomfort in **Pyramids of Mars**.*

Exxilon City Antibodies
*Are immune to the Daleks' machine-guns in **Death to the Daleks**.*

The Haemovores
*Are not bothered by British or Russian gunfire in **The Curse of Fenric**.*

I'D RATHER HAVE A PINT

This is one of the Brigadier's best-known orders, even if it isn't exactly a military one. In **The Green Death**, the Brigadier tells a stroppy Doctor, 'I wouldn't like to have to order you, Doctor.' The Doctor replies: 'I wouldn't advise you to try.' But here are some of the more outlandish orders the Brigadier has given.

- 'Jenkins – chap with wings there, five rounds rapid.'

  Perhaps the Brig's most famous order of all from **The Daemons**.

- 'Lay on a coffee.'

  A cheeky suggestion made to Corporal Bell in **The Mind of Evil**. *'Lay on a Jeep,' is also an order which the Brig is not ashamed to give to Benton.*

- 'Doctor, come back at once!'

  A dangerous thing to shout, given that the Brigadier is now standing exactly where the TARDIS has gone from in **Colony in Space**.

- 'Get off my world!'

  The Brigadier's order to the Destroyer before he shoots it dead.

- 'Fire at will!'

  Used on various occasions (for example, **Invasion of the Dinosaurs**) *and proof positive that there are no UNIT personnel called William. None living, anyway.*

- 'Be quiet, Sir!'

  The Brig demonstrates his diplomatic skills to Sir Reginald Styles in **Day of the Daleks**.

HERE WE GO AGAIN

Inevitably perhaps on such a long-running programme, the same title has been used more than once for a story or episode. Here are the gaffs, as well as some near-misses.

The Mutants

*The production office title of the first Dalek story (more usually called **The Daleks**, luckily) and the Pertwee story of the same name.*

Inferno

*Another Pertwee story, as well as the final episode of **The Romans**.*

The Dimensions of Time

*An episode of **The Chase** that's a hair's-breadth away from **Dimensions in Time**, so lucky that's not a 'real' story.*

Return of the Cybermen

*The working title for both **The Invasion** and **Revenge of the Cybermen**.*

Invasion

*Episode one of **Invasion of the Dinosaurs** was titled simply **Invasion**, as was episode five of **The Web Planet**. **The Invasion** comes close.*

The Space Pirates

*Almost – **The Pirate Planet** had this as a working title, according to some sources.*

The Enemy Within

*Doesn't count at all. The story with this as a working title became the less accurate **The Invisible Enemy**, the Christopher Priest story with this title was never made, and though it's used for **Doctor Who: The Movie**, there's no real basis for this in the production cycle or broadcast programme.*

IN A WORD...

A straightforward list of one-word episode and story titles. So straightforward we decided **Time-Flight** was not eligible.

Episodes

Crisis	Invasion
Flashpoint	Checkmate
Inferno	Airlock
Kidnap	Volcano
Conspiracy	Invasion *(part one of **Invasion of the Dinosaurs**)*

Stories

Inferno	Logopolis	Frontios
Robot	Castrovalva	Timelash
Underworld	Earthshock	Dragonfire
Shada	Snakedance	Battlefield
Meglos	Enlightenment	Survival

DASH IT ALL

Another straightforward list – this time of episodes and stories which include some form of punctuation in their story titles.

Episodes	Stories
Rider From Shang-Tu	100,000 BC
World's End	The Daleks' Master Plan
Small Prophet, Quick Return	Warriors' Gate
Devil's Planet	Time-Flight
Don't Shoot the Pianist	The King's Demons

IT'S STILL JUST A POLICE BOX

Or is it? The TARDIS has a chameleon circuit which, in theory, it uses to change its shape to blend in with its surroundings. Here are the shapes we have seen a TARDIS assume. Shapes we are told it has, or could assume are not included (Ionic column and sedan chair mentioned in **100,000 BC**, Howdah mentioned in **The Time Meddler**, Pyramid shown on scanner in **Logopolis**). Nor have we included the Rani's TARDIS masquerading as the Queen Vic pub in Albert Square from **Dimensions In Time**.

The Doctor's TARDIS

- Police box – **100,000 BC** onwards.
- Cabinet – **Attack of the Cybermen**.
- Organ – **Attack of the Cybermen**.
- Gate – **Attack of the Cybermen**.

The Master's TARDIS

- Horsebox – **Terror of the Autons**.
- Spaceship – **Colony in Space**.
- Computer bank – **The Time Monster**.
- Grandfather clock – **The Deadly Assassin, The Keeper of Traken**.
- Melkur – **The Keeper of Traken**.
- Police box – **Logopolis**.
- Ionic column – **Logopolis, Castrovalva**.
- Potted shrub – **Logopolis**.
- Fireplace – **Castrovalva**.
- Iron maiden – **The King's Demons**.
- Trion/Sarn obelisk – **Planet of Fire**.

- Statue of Queen Victoria – **The Trial of a Time Lord.**
- Beach hut – **The Trial of a Time Lord.**

The Monk's TARDIS

- Saxon sarcophagus – **The Time Meddler.**
- Motorbike – **The Daleks' Master Plan.**
- Police box – **The Daleks' Master Plan.**
- Not very convincing block of ice – **The Daleks' Master Plan.**

Chronotis' TARDIS

- A study – **Shada.**

Omega's TARDIS

- Sepulchre – **Arc of Infinity.**

The Rani's TARDIS

- Cupboard – **Mark of the Rani.**
- Pyramid – **Time and the Rani.**

THE NAKED TRUTH

While **Doctor Who** is a family show, that has not prevented the occasional glimpse of (gasp) naked flesh or underclothing. To save you hunting through your videos on fast-search, here's a quick guide. We have not included invisible or nude non-humanoids (even Daleks), though the Sea Devils deserve a special mention for those tasteful string vests with which they hide their modesty. Alpha Centauri, even with the cape, defies description.

100,000 BC
The tribe are rather short on clothing, despite the cold weather.

The Daleks
The Thals could wrap up a bit as well.

The Romans
Galley slaves and others strip to the waist to keep (and appear) cool.

The Crusade
Ian staked out in the desert and daubed with honey so the ants will eat him.

The Daleks' Master Plan
The ancient Egyptians.

The Underwater Menace
Bathing beauties and fish people.

The Evil of the Daleks
Kemel shows off his attributes in a test of strength.

Spearhead from Space
The Doctor has a shower wearing only a shower cap and showing off his snake tattoo.

Terror of the Autons
Rossini's circus strongman sports a neat leopard-skin top.

The Curse of Peladon and **The Monster of Peladon**
Leather halter-tops for the guards. Makes them seem butch and scary, one supposes.

The Time Monster
Near-naked Atlanteans, and baby Benton stepping out of his nappy when he returns to his real age and size at the end of the story.

Planet of the Daleks
The invisible Spiridons, when not wearing their purple gowns, are, one supposes, completely naked. (Other invisible races are not included as we don't know if they are humanoid — we know that the Spiridons are, as we see Wester become visible when he dies.)

The Green Death

Cliff Jones naked (and green) in bed as Jo ministers to his ills.

Death to the Daleks

Sarah all decked out for a sunbathe before they arrive on Exxilon. Bellal and his underground Exxilons are distinguishable from other Exxilons by having paler skin — and not wearing the chamois-leather gear.

The Brain of Morbius

Morbius (well, he was humanoid originally).

The Seeds of Doom

Both Winlett and Keeler as they mutate into Krynoids.

Face of Evil

The Sevateem are a generally immodest lot with a leather fixation.

Leela

*Dashing round in leather in all stories between **Face of Evil** and **The Invasion of Time**, except **The Talons of Weng-Chiang** (where she runs through the London sewers in wet underwear) and **Horror of Fang Rock** (when she says 'I'm no lady,' and then strips off in front of Vince).*

The Power of Kroll

The Swampies do their Jolly Green Giant impressions.

Full Circle

The swimmers retrieving river fruits wear only tasteful yellow loin-cloths.

Kinda

Loin-cloths and wraparounds galore for the tribe.

Black Orchid

The Doctor in a dressing gown.

Snakedance

Dojjen.

Terminus

Nyssa in skimpy chemise, and removing her skirt.

Planet of Fire

Turlough and Peri in (just) their swim things.

Vengeance on Varos

Torture scenes in which viewers are forced to watch Jason Connery's bare chest get spotlit. The cannibals are also short on clothing.

Doctor Who: The Movie

The Doctor is stripped down for his operation and subsequently regenerates wearing only a toe tag. Not to be outdone, the Master shows off his new body at Bruce's bedroom window.

IT'S A SCREAM

Doctor Who is often a scream for the companions, so here are some of the very best screams ever in the programme.

- Barbara's scream at the first sight of a Dalek (**The Daleks**).

- Victoria screaming to destroy the seaweed creature – much more convincing than the original idea of having Jamie play the bagpipes (**Fury from the Deep**).

- Mel giving it her all in **Time and the Rani**.

- Professor Laird (Chloe Ashcroft) exterminated in **Resurrection of the Daleks**.

- Mel screams into the closing theme music at the close of part nine of **The Trial of a Time Lord**.

- Jane Hampden catches a glimpse of the Malus (end of part one of **The Awakening**).

- Jo fakes an attack of the heebie-jeebies to lure in the Ogron guard (**Day of the Daleks**).

- The Doctor apparently pitches to his death as he walks the plank (**The Pirate Planet**).

- Lady Adrasta is less than happy that Erato is about to find his voice (**The Creature from the Pit**).

- Vogel is exterminated (**Revelation of the Daleks**).

- Adelaide Lessage screams at anything that moves throughout **Horror of Fang Rock**.

- Ronson gives it all he's got as he becomes the first victim of the Daleks (**Genesis of the Daleks**).

- The fortune-teller, otherwise less than convincing, turns in an excellent scream when unforeseen things appear in her crystal ball (**Snakedance**).

. . . ON A NAMELESS PLANET

Just to make it a bit easier, here are the stories in which unnamed planets appear. That's easier for you and us than listing the planets.

The Keys of Marinus
If Marinus is the island, as Arbitan's map implies, and not the planet.

Galaxy 4

The Daleks' Master Plan
An ice planet where the Monk is stranded.

The Savages

The Macra Terror

The Krotons

The War Games
The planet where the games are carried out, plus the aliens' home planet. The Time Lord planet is also not named in this story, though we later discover it to be Gallifrey.

The Three Doctors
If Omega's world counts.

Frontier in Space
The Ogron home planet is never named.

Face of Evil
The Doctor refers to the Mordee expedition, but whether Mordee is the planet, the intended destination which may be different, the race that sent the ship, the name of the ship, or something else is never stated.

Robots of Death
Reference to Kaldor City, but the planet is not named.

Image of the Fendahl
The home of the Fendahl, described as the 'fifth planet'.

Underworld

Castrovalva
Is the settlement (not the planet), also known as Dwellings of Simplicity.

Paradise Towers
Could be set on Earth, even.

Survival
The planet is referred to imaginatively as the 'Planet of the Cheetah People'.

WHAT A STUPID PLACE TO LAND...

Over the centuries, the Doctor's TARDIS has landed in some strange and unusual places... Some more unusual than others.

- On its side
  The Ice Warriors, Castrovalva.

- Right on the edge of a cliff
  *End of **The Rescue** / start of **The Romans**, **The Curse of Peladon**.*

- No time, no place
  *The gateway between the universes (**Warriors' Gate**).*

- The Land of Fiction
  The Mind Robber.

- On water
  Fury from the Deep, The War Games.

- Exactly where it was, but hundreds of years later
  The Ark.

- In space
  The Web of Fear, The War Games, Underworld, The Horns of Nimon, Four to Doomsday...

- Between two paving stones on a path
  Planet of Giants.

- A rubbish tip
  Inferno – console only.

- Invisibly
  The Invasion.

- The hydrogen in-rush that started the galaxy, Event One
  Castrovalva.

- The start of the universe, perhaps
  Inside the Spaceship.

BY POPULAR DEMAND

Repeats on BBC television are not unusual these days, even occasional repeats of **Doctor Who**. That said there are many stories that have never been repeated. Others seem to have been shown by the BBC more than their fair share.

An Unearthly Child

*The very first episode was repeated the following week before the second episode (except in Northern Ireland). The whole story **100,000 BC** was reshown as part of the **Five Faces of Doctor Who** season in 1981. An edited version of the pilot version of the first episode was also shown in August 1991.*

The Daemons

A 90-minute Christmas omnibus repeat in 1971 (setting a trend for a few years), and a repeat broadcast of the full story (restored to colour by whizzo BBC technology) in 1992.

The Sea Devils

Repeated as a 90-minute compilation in December 1972. The compilation was also shown as a replacement for rained-off cricket in 1974, and the story was repeated in its entirety in 1992.

The Green Death

A 90-minute compilation repeat in December 1973, and a full repeat in 1994.

Genesis of the Daleks

*A 90-minute compilation repeat in December 1975, plus an airing in two fifty-minute parts as part of **Doctor Who and the Monsters** in 1982. It later got a repeat in its full episodic glory.*

Pyramids of Mars

Shown as an hour-long compilation in 1976 and also repeated in full in 1994.

APPENDIX

THE BASICS

THE STORIES

Story code	Story title		Episode number/Episode title (if there is one)		Transmission date

Season 1

A	**(100,000 BC)**	1	An Unearthly Child		23/11/63
A		2	The Cave of Skulls		30/11/63
A		3	The Forest of Fear		7/12/63
A		4	The Firemaker		14/12/63
B	**(The Mutants**	1	The Dead Planet		21/12/63
B	aka **The Daleks)**	2	The Survivors		28/12/63
B		3	The Escape		4/1/64
B		4	The Ambush		11/1/64
B		5	The Expedition		18/1/64
B		6	The Ordeal		25/1/64
B		7	The Rescue		1/2/64
C	**(Inside the Spaceship)**	1	The Edge of Destruction		8/2/64
C		2	The Brink of Disaster		15/2/64
D	**(Marco Polo)**	1	The Roof of the World		22/2/64
D		2	The Singing Sands		29/2/64
D		3	Five Hundred Eyes		7/3/64
D		4	The Wall of Lies		14/3/64
D		5	Rider from Shang-tu		21/3/64
D		6	Mighty Kublai Khan		28/3/64
D		7	Assassin at Peking		4/4/64
E	**(The Keys of Marinus)**	1	The Sea of Death		11/4/64
E		2	The Velvet Web		18/4/64
E		3	The Screaming Jungle		25/4/64
E		4	The Snows of Terror		2/5/64
E		5	Sentence of Death		9/5/64
E		6	The Keys of Marinus		16/5/64
F	**(The Aztecs)**	1	The Temple of Evil		23/5/64
F		2	The Warriors of Death		30/5/64
F		3	The Bride of Sacrifice		6/6/64
F		4	The Day of Darkness		13/6/64
G	**(The Sensorites)**	1	Strangers in Space		20/6/64
G		2	The Unwilling Warriors		27/6/64
G		3	Hidden Danger		11/7/64
G		4	A Race Against Death		18/7/64
G		5	Kidnap		25/7/64
G		6	A Desperate Venture		1/8/64
H	**(The Reign of Terror)**	1	A Land of Fear		8/8/64

H		2	Guests of Madame Guillotine	15/8/64
H		3	A Change of Identity	22/8/64
H		4	The Tyrant of France	29/8/64
H		5	A Bargain of Necessity	5/9/64
H		6	Prisoners of Conciergerie	12/9/64

Season 2

J	**(Planet of Giants)**	1	Planet of Giants	31/10/64
J		2	Dangerous Journey	7/11/64
J		3	Crisis	14/11/64
K	**(The Dalek Invasion**	1	World's End	21/11/64
K	**of Earth)**	2	The Daleks	28/11/64
K		3	Day of Reckoning	5/12/64
K		4	The End of Tomorrow	12/12/64
K		5	The Waking Ally	19/12/64
K		6	Flashpoint	26/12/64
L	**(The Rescue)**	1	The Powerful Enemy	2/1/65
L		2	Desperate Measures	9/1/65
M	**(The Romans)**	1	The Slave Traders	16/1/65
M		2	All Roads Lead to Rome	23/1/65
M		3	Conspiracy	30/1/65
M		4	Inferno	6/2/65
N	**(The Web Planet)**	1	The Web Planet	13/2/65
N		2	The Zarbi	20/2/65
N		3	Escape to Danger	27/2/65
N		4	Crater of Needles	6/3/65
N		5	Invasion	13/3/65
N		6	The Centre	20/3/65
P	**(The Crusade)**	1	The Lion	27/3/65
P		2	The Knight of Jaffa	3/4/65
P		3	The Wheel of Fortune	10/4/65
P		4	The Warlords	17/4/65
Q	**(The Space Museum)**	1	The Space Museum	24/4/65
Q		2	The Dimensions of Time	1/5/65
Q		3	The Search	8/5/65
Q		4	The Final Phase	15/5/65
R	**(The Chase)**	1	The Executioners	22/5/65
R		2	The Death of Time	29/5/65
R		3	Flight Through Eternity	5/6/65
R		4	Journey Into Terror	12/6/65
R		5	The Death of Doctor Who	19/6/65
R		6	Planet of Decision	26/6/65
S	**(The Time Meddler)**	1	The Watcher	3/7/65
S		2	The Meddling Monk	10/7/65
S		3	A Battle of Wits	17/7/65
S		4	Checkmate	24/7/65

T	**(Galaxy 4)**	1	Four Hundred Dawns	11/9/65
T		2	Trap of Steel	18/9/65
T		3	Air Lock	25/9/65
T		4	The Exploding Planet	2/10/65
T/A	**(Dalek Cutaway)**	1	Mission to the Unknown	9/10/65
U	**(The Myth Makers)**	1	Temple of Secrets	16/10/65
U		2	Small Prophet, Quick Return	23/10/65
U		3	Death of a Spy	30/10/65
U		4	Horse of Destruction	6/11/65
V	**(The Daleks'**	1	The Nightmare Begins	13/11/65
V	**Master Plan)**	2	Day of Armageddon	20/11/65
V		3	Devil's Planet	27/11/65
V		4	The Traitors	4/12/65
V		5	Counter Plot	11/12/65
V		6	Coronas of the Sun	18/12/65
V		7	The Feast of Steven	25/12/65
V		8	Volcano	1/1/66
V		9	Golden Death	8/1/66
V		10	Escape Switch	15/1/66
V		11	The Abandoned Planet	22/1/66
V		12	The Destruction of Time	29/1/66
W	**(The Massacre of**	1	War of God	5/2/66
	St Bartholomew's Eve)			
W		2	The Sea Beggar	12/2/66
W		3	Priest of Death	19/2/66
W		4	Bell of Doom	26/2/66
X	**(The Ark)**	1	The Steel Sky	5/3/66
X		2	The Plague	12/3/66
X		3	The Return	19/3/66
X		4	The Bomb	26/3/66
Y	**(The Celestial**	1	The Celestial Toyroom	2/4/66
	Toymaker)			
Y		2	The Hall of Dolls	9/4/66
Y		3	The Dancing Floor	16/4/66
Y		4	The Final Test	23/4/66
Z	**(The Gunfighters)**	1	A Holiday for the Doctor	30/4/66
Z		2	Don't Shoot the Pianist	7/5/66
Z		3	Johnny Ringo	14/5/66
Z		4	The OK Corral	21/5/66
AA	**The Savages**		Episode 1	28/5/66
AA			Episode 2	4/6/66
AA			Episode 3	11/6/66
AA			Episode 4	18/6/66
BB	**The War Machines**		Episode 1	25/6/66

BB		Episode 2	2/7/66
BB		Episode 3	9/7/66
BB		Episode 4	16/7/66
Season 4			
CC	**The Smugglers**	Episode 1	10/9/66
CC		Episode 2	17/9/66
CC		Episode 3	24/9/66
CC		Episode 4	1/10/66
DD	**The Tenth Planet**	Episode 1	8/10/66
DD		Episode 2	15/10/66
DD		Episode 3	22/10/66
DD		Episode 4	29/10/66
EE	**The Power of the Daleks**	Episode 1	5/11/66
EE		Episode 2	12/11/66
EE		Episode 3	19/11/66
EE		Episode 4	26/11/66
EE		Episode 5	3/12/66
EE		Episode 6	10/12/66
FF	**The Highlanders**	Episode 1	17/12/66
FF		Episode 2	24/12/66
FF		Episode 3	31/12/66
FF		Episode 4	7/1/67
GG	**The Underwater Menace**	Episode 1	14/1/67
GG		Episode 2	21/1/67
GG		Episode 3	28/1/67
GG		Episode 4	4/2/67
HH	**The Moonbase**	Episode 1	11/2/67
HH		Episode 2	18/2/67
HH		Episode 3	25/2/67
HH		Episode 4	4/3/67
JJ	**The Macra Terror**	Episode 1	11/3/67
JJ		Episode 2	18/3/67
JJ		Episode 3	25/3/67
JJ		Episode 4	1/4/67
KK	**The Faceless Ones**	Episode 1	8/4/67
KK		Episode 2	15/4/67
KK		Episode 3	22/4/67
KK		Episode 4	29/4/67
KK		Episode 5	6/5/67
KK		Episode 6	13/5/67
LL	**The Evil of the Daleks**	Episode 1	20/5/67
LL		Episode 2	27/5/67
LL		Episode 3	3/6/67
LL		Episode 4	10/6/67
LL		Episode 5	17/6/67

LL		Episode 6	24/6/67
LL		Episode 7	1/7/67

MM	**The Tomb of the Cybermen**	Episode 1	2/9/67
MM		Episode 2	9/9/67
MM		Episode 3	16/9/67
MM		Episode 4	23/9/67
NN	**The Abominable Snowmen**	Episode One	30/9/67
NN		Episode Two	7/10/67
NN		Episode Three	14/10/67
NN		Episode Four	21/10/67
NN		Episode Five	28/10/67
NN		Episode Six	4/11/67
OO	**The Ice Warriors**	One	11/11/67
OO		Two	18/11/67
OO		Three	25/11/67
OO		Four	2/12/67
OO		Five	9/12/67
OO		Six	16/12/67
PP	**The Enemy of the World**	Episode 1	23/12/67
PP		Episode 2	30/12/67
PP		Episode 3	6/1/68
PP		Episode 4	13/1/68
PP		Episode 5	20/1/68
PP		Episode 6	27/1/68
QQ	**The Web of Fear**	Episode 1	3/2/68
QQ		Episode 2	10/2/68
QQ		Episode 3	17/2/68
QQ		Episode 4	24/2/68
QQ		Episode 5	2/3/68
QQ		Episode 6	9/3/68
RR	**Fury from the Deep**	Episode 1	16/3/68
RR		Episode 2	23/3/68
RR		Episode 3	30/3/68
RR		Episode 4	6/4/68
RR		Episode 5	13/4/68
RR		Episode 6	20/4/68
SS	**The Wheel in Space**	Episode 1	27/4/68
SS		Episode 2	4/5/68
SS		Episode 3	11/5/68
SS		Episode 4	18/5/68
SS		Episode 5	25/5/68
SS		Episode 6	1/6/68

TT	**The Dominators**	Episode 1	10/8/68
TT		Episode 2	17/8/68
TT		Episode 3	24/8/68
TT		Episode 4	31/8/68
TT		Episode 5	7/9/68
UU	**The Mind Robber**	Episode 1	14/9/68
UU		Episode 2	21/9/68
UU		Episode 3	28/9/68
UU		Episode 4	5/10/68
UU		Episode 5	12/10/68
VV	**The Invasion**	Episode One	2/11/68
VV		Episode Two	9/11/68
VV		Episode Three	16/11/68
VV		Episode Four	23/11/68
VV		Episode Five	30/11/68
VV		Episode Six	7/12/68
VV		Episode Seven	14/12/68
VV		Episode Eight	21/12/68
WW	**The Krotons**	Episode One	28/12/68
WW		Episode Two	4/1/69
WW		Episode Three	11/1/69
WW		Episode Four	18/1/69
XX	**The Seeds of Death**	Episode One	25/1/69
XX		Episode Two	1/2/69
XX		Episode Three	8/2/69
XX		Episode Four	15/2/69
XX		Episode Five	22/2/69
XX		Episode Six	1/3/69
YY	**The Space Pirates**	Episode One	8/3/69
YY		Episode Two	15/3/69
YY		Episode Three	22/3/69
YY		Episode Four	29/3/69
YY		Episode Five	5/4/69
YY		Episode Six	12/4/69
ZZ	**The War Games**	Episode One	19/4/69
ZZ		Episode Two	26/4/69
ZZ		Episode Three	3/5/69
ZZ		Episode Four	10/5/69
ZZ		Episode Five	17/5/69
ZZ		Episode Six	24/5/69
ZZ		Episode Seven	31/5/69
ZZ		Episode Eight	7/6/69
ZZ		Episode Nine	14/6/69
ZZ		Episode Ten	21/6/69

Season 7

AAA	**Spearhead from Space**	Episode 1	3/1/70
AAA		Episode 2	10/1/70
AAA		Episode 3	17/1/70
AAA		Episode 4	24/1/70
BBB	**Doctor Who and the Silurians**	Episode 1	31/1/70
BBB		Episode 2	7/2/70
BBB		Episode 3	14/2/70
BBB		Episode 4	21/2/70
BBB		Episode 5	28/2/70
BBB		Episode 6	7/3/70
BBB		Episode 7	14/3/70
CCC	**The Ambassadors of Death**	Episode 1	21/3/70
CCC		Episode 2	28/3/70
CCC		Episode 3	4/4/70
CCC		Episode 4	11/4/70
CCC		Episode 5	18/4/70
CCC		Episode 6	25/4/70
CCC		Episode 7	2/5/70
DDD	**Inferno**	Episode 1	9/5/70
DDD		Episode 2	16/5/70
DDD		Episode 3	23/5/70
DDD		Episode 4	30/5/70
DDD		Episode 5	6/6/70
DDD		Episode 6	13/6/70
DDD		Episode 7	20/6/70

Season 8

EEE	**Terror of the Autons**	Episode One	2/1/71
EEE		Episode Two	9/1/71
EEE		Episode Three	16/1/71
EEE		Episode Four	23/1/71
FFF	**The Mind of Evil**	Episode One	30/1/71
FFF		Episode Two	6/2/71
FFF		Episode Three	13/2/71
FFF		Episode Four	20/2/71
FFF		Episode Five	27/2/71
FFF		Episode Six	6/3/71
GGG	**The Claws of Axos**	Episode One	13/3/71
GGG		Episode Two	20/3/71
GGG		Episode Three	27/3/71
GGG		Episode Four	3/4/71
HHH	**Colony in Space**	Episode One	10/4/71
HHH		Episode Two	17/4/71

HHH		Episode Three	24/4/71
HHH		Episode Four	1/5/71
HHH		Episode Five	8/5/71
HHH		Episode Six	15/5/71
JJJ	**The Daemons**	Episode One	22/5/71
JJJ		Episode Two	29/5/71
JJJ		Episode Three	5/6/71
JJJ		Episode Four	12/6/71
JJJ		Episode Five	19/6/71

Season 9

KKK	**Day of the Daleks**	Episode One	1/1/72
KKK		Episode Two	8/1/72
KKK		Episode Three	15/1/72
KKK		Episode Four	22/1/72
MMM	**The Curse of Peladon**	Episode One	29/1/72
MMM		Episode Two	5/2/72
MMM		Episode Three	12/2/72
MMM		Episode Four	19/2/72
LLL	**The Sea Devils**	Episode One	26/2/72
LLL		Episode Two	4/3/72
LLL		Episode Three	11/3/72
LLL		Episode Four	18/3/72
LLL		Episode Five	25/3/72
LLL		Episode Six	1/4/72
NNN	**The Mutants**	Episode One	8/4/72
NNN		Episode Two	15/4/72
NNN		Episode Three	22/4/72
NNN		Episode Four	29/4/72
NNN		Episode Five	6/5/72
NNN		Episode Six	13/5/72
OOO	**The Time Monster**	Episode One	20/5/72
OOO		Episode Two	27/5/72
OOO		Episode Three	3/6/72
OOO		Episode Four	10/6/72
OOO		Episode Five	17/6/72
OOO		Episode Six	24/6/72

Season 10

RRR	**The Three Doctors**	Episode One	30/12/72
RRR		Episode Two	6/1/73
RRR		Episode Three	13/1/73
RRR		Episode Four	20/1/73
PPP	**Carnival of Monsters**	Episode One	27/1/73
PPP		Episode Two	3/2/73
PPP		Episode Three	10/2/73
PPP		Episode Four	17/2/73

QQQ	Frontier in Space	Episode One	24/2/73
QQQ		Episode Two	3/3/73
QQQ		Episode Three	10/3/73
QQQ		Episode Four	17/3/73
QQQ		Episode Five	24/3/73
QQQ		Episode Six	31/3/73
SSS	**Planet of the Daleks**	Episode One	7/4/73
SSS		Episode Two	14/4/73
SSS		Episode Three	21/4/73
SSS		Episode Four	28/4/73
SSS		Episode Five	5/5/73
SSS		Episode Six	12/5/73
TTT	**The Green Death**	Episode One	19/5/73
TTT		Episode Two	26/5/73
TTT		Episode Three	2/6/73
TTT		Episode Four	9/6/73
TTT		Episode Five	16/6/73
TTT		Episode Six	23/6/73
Season 11			
UUU	**The Time Warrior**	Part One	15/12/73
UUU		Part Two	22/12/73
UUU		Part Three	29/12/73
UUU		Part Four	5/1/74
WWW	**Invasion**	Part One	12/1/74
WWW	**Invasion of the Dinosaurs**	Part Two	19/1/74
WWW		Part Three	26/1/74
WWW		Part Four	2/2/74
WWW		Part Five	9/2/74
WWW		Part Six	16/2/74
XXX	**Death to the Daleks**	Part One	23/2/74
XXX		Part Two	2/3/74
XXX		Part Three	9/3/74
XXX		Part Four	16/3/74
YYY	**The Monster of Peladon**	Part One	23/3/74
YYY		Part Two	30/3/74
YYY		Part Three	6/4/74
YYY		Part Four	13/4/74
YYY		Part Five	20/4/74
YYY		Part Six	27/4/74
ZZZ	**Planet of the Spiders**	Part One	4/5/74
ZZZ		Part Two	11/5/74
ZZZ		Part Three	18/5/74
ZZZ		Part Four	25/5/74
ZZZ		Part Five	1/6/74
ZZZ		Part Six	8/6/74

4A	**Robot**	Part One	28/12/74
4A		Part Two	4/1/75
4A		Part Three	11/1/75
4A		Part Four	18/1/75
4C	**The Ark in Space**	Part One	25/1/75
4C		Part Two	1/2/75
4C		Part Three	8/2/75
4C		Part Four	15/2/75
4B	**The Sontaran Experiment**	Part One	22/2/75
4B		Part Two	1/3/75
4E	**Genesis of the Daleks**	Part One	8/3/75
4E		Part Two	15/3/75
4E		Part Three	22/3/75
4E		Part Four	29/3/75
4E		Part Five	5/4/75
4E		Part Six	12/4/75
4D	**Revenge of the Cybermen**	Part One	19/4/75
4D		Part Two	26/4/75
4D		Part Three	3/5/75
4D		Part Four	10/5/75

Season 13

4F	**Terror of the Zygons**	Part One	30/8/75
4F		Part Two	6/9/75
4F		Part Three	13/9/75
4F		Part Four	20/9/75
4H	**Planet of Evil**	Part One	27/9/75
4H		Part Two	4/10/75
4H		Part Three	11/10/75
4H		Part Four	18/10/75
4G	**Pyramids of Mars**	Part One	25/10/75
4G		Part Two	1/11/75
4G		Part Three	8/11/75
4G		Part Four	15/11/75
4J	**The Android Invasion**	Part One	22/11/75
4J		Part Two	29/11/75
4J		Part Three	6/12/75
4J		Part Four	13/12/75
4K	**The Brain of Morbius**	Part One	3/1/76
4K		Part Two	10/1/76
4K		Part Three	17/1/76
4K		Part Four	24/1/76
4L	**The Seeds of Doom**	Part One	31/1/76

4L		Part Two	7/2/76
4L		Part Three	14/2/76
4L		Part Four	21/2/76
4L		Part Five	28/2/76
4L		Part Six	6/3/76

Season 14

4M	**The Masque of Mandragora**	Part One	4/9/76
4M		Part Two	11/9/76
4M		Part Three	18/9/76
4M		Part Four	25/9/76
4N	**The Hand of Fear**	Part One	2/10/76
4N		Part Two	9/10/76
4N		Part Three	16/10/76
4N		Part Four	23/10/76
4P	**The Deadly Assassin**	Part One	30/10/76
4P		Part Two	6/11/76
4P		Part Three	13/11/76
4P		Part Four	20/11/76
4Q	**The Face of Evil**	Part One	1/1/77
4Q		Part Two	8/1/77
4Q		Part Three	15/1/77
4Q		Part Four	22/1/77
4R	**The Robots of Death**	Part One	29/1/77
4R		Part Two	5/2/77
4R		Part Three	12/2/77
4R		Part Four	19/2/77
4S	**The Talons of Weng-Chiang**	Part One	26/2/77
4S		Part Two	5/3/77
4S		Part Three	12/3/77
4S		Part Four	19/3/77
4S		Part Five	26/3/77
4S		Part Six	2/4/77

Season 15

4V	**Horror of Fang Rock**	Part One	3/9/77
4V		Part Two	10/9/77
4V		Part Three	17/9/77
4V		Part Four	24/9/77
4T	**The Invisible Enemy**	Part One	1/10/77
4T		Part Two	8/10/77
4T		Part Three	15/10/77
4T		Part Four	22/10/77
4X	**Image of the Fendahl**	Part One	29/10/77
4X		Part Two	5/11/77

4X		Part Three	12/11/77
4X		Part Four	19/11/77
4W	**The Sun Makers**	Part One	26/11/77
4W		Part Two	3/12/77
4W		Part Three	10/12/77
4W		Part Four	17/12/77
4Y	**Underworld**	Part One	7/1/78
4Y		Part Two	14/1/78
4Y		Part Three	21/1/78
4Y		Part Four	28/1/78
4Z	**The Invasion of Time**	Part One	4/2/78
4Z		Part Two	11/2/78
4Z		Part Three	18/2/78
4Z		Part Four	25/2/78
4Z		Part Five	4/3/78
4Z		Part Six	11/3/78

Season 16

5A	**The Ribos Operation**	Part One	2/9/78
5A		Part Two	9/9/78
5A		Part Three	16/9/78
5A		Part Four	23/9/78
5B	**The Pirate Planet**	Part One	30/9/78
5B		Part Two	7/10/78
5B		Part Three	14/10/78
5B		Part Four	21/10/78
5C	**The Stones of Blood**	Part One	28/10/78
5C		Part Two	4/11/78
5C		Part Three	11/11/78
5C		Part Four	18/11/78
5D	**The Androids of Tara**	Part One	25/11/78
5D		Part Two	2/12/78
5D		Part Three	9/12/78
5D		Part Four	16/12/78
5E	**The Power of Kroll**	Part One	23/12/78
5E		Part Two	30/12/78
5E		Part Three	6/1/79
5E		Part Four	13/1/79
5F	**The Armageddon Factor**	Part One	20/1/79
5F		Part Two	27/1/79
5F		Part Three	3/2/79
5F		Part Four	10/2/79
5F		Part Five	17/2/79
5F		Part Six	24/2/79

Season 17

5J	**Destiny of the Daleks**	Episode One	1/9/79

211

5J		Episode Two	8/9/79
5J		Episode Three	15/9/79
5J		Episode Four	22/9/79
5H	**City of Death**	Part One	29/9/79
5H		Part Two	6/10/79
5H		Part Three	13/10/79
5H		Part Four	20/10/79
5G	**The Creature from the Pit**	Part One	27/10/79
5G		Part Two	3/11/79
5G		Part Three	10/11/79
5G		Part Four	17/11/79
5K	**Nightmare of Eden**	Part One	24/11/79
5K		Part Two	1/12/79
5K		Part Three	8/12/79
5K		Part Four	15/12/79
5L	**The Horns of Nimon**	Part One	22/12/79
5L		Part Two	29/12/79
5L		Part Three	5/1/80
5L		Part Four	12/1/80

Serial 5M, Shada was only partially completed and never broadcast. Proposed dates were:

5M	**Shada**	Part One	19/1/80
5M		Part Two	26/1/80
5M		Part Three	2/2/80
5M		Part Four	9/2/80
5M		Part Five	16/2/80
5M		Part Six	23/2/80

Season 18

5N	**The Leisure Hive**	Part One	30/8/80
5N		Part Two	6/9/80
5N		Part Three	13/9/80
5N		Part Four	20/9/80
5Q	**Meglos**	Part One	27/9/80
5Q		Part Two	4/10/80
5Q		Part Three	11/10/80
5Q		Part Four	18/10/80
5R	**Full Circle**	Part One	25/10/80
5R		Part Two	1/11/80
5R		Part Three	8/11/80
5R		Part Four	15/11/80
5P	**State of Decay**	Part One	22/11/80
5P		Part Two	29/11/80
5P		Part Three	6/12/80
5P		Part Four	13/12/80
5S	**Warriors' Gate**	Part One	3/1/81

5S		Part Two	10/1/81
5S		Part Three	17/1/81
5S		Part Four	24/1/81
5T	**The Keeper of Traken**	Part One	31/1/81
5T		Part Two	7/2/81
5T		Part Three	14/2/81
5T		Part Four	21/2/81
5V	**Logopolis**	Part One	28/2/81
5V		Part Two	7/3/81
5V		Part Three	14/3/81
5V		Part Four	21/3/81
(K9 and Company (pilot)		A Girl's Best Friend	28/12/81)

Season 19

5Z	**Castrovalva**	Part One	4/1/82
5Z		Part Two	5/1/82
5Z		Part Three	11/1/82
5Z		Part Four	12/1/82
5W	**Four to Doomsday**	Part One	18/1/82
5W		Part Two	19/1/82
5W		Part Three	25/1/82
5W		Part Four	26/1/82
5Y	**Kinda**	Part One	1/2/82
5Y		Part Two	2/2/82
5Y		Part Three	8/2/82
5Y		Part Four	9/2/82
5X	**The Visitation**	Part One	15/2/82
5X		Part Two	16/2/82
5X		Part Three	22/2/82
5X		Part Four	23/2/82
6A	**Black Orchid**	Part One	1/3/82
6A		Part Two	2/3/82
6B	**Earthshock**	Part One	8/3/82
6B		Part Two	9/3/82
6B		Part Three	15/3/82
6B		Part Four	16/3/82
6C	**Time-Flight**	Part One	22/3/82
6C		Part Two	23/3/82
6C		Part Three	29/3/82
6C		Part Four	30/3/82

Season 20

6E	**Arc of Infinity**	Part One	3/1/83
6E		Part Two	5/1/83
6E		Part Three	11/1/83

6E		Part Four	12/1/83
6D	**Snakedance**	Part One	18/1/83
6D		Part Two	19/1/83
6D		Part Three	25/1/83
6D		Part Four	26/1/83
6F	**Mawdryn Undead**	Part One	1/2/83
6F		Part Two	2/2/83
6F		Part Three	8/2/83
6F		Part Four	9/2/83
6G	**Terminus**	Part One	15/2/83
6G		Part Two	16/2/83
6G		Part Three	22/2/83
6G		Part Four	23/2/83
6H	**Enlightenment**	Part One	1/3/83
6H		Part Two	2/3/83
6H		Part Three	8/3/83
6H		Part Four	9/3/83
6J	**The King's Demons**	Part One	15/3/83
6J		Part Two	16/3/83
6K	**The Five Doctors**		25/11/83

Season 21

6L	**Warriors of the Deep**	Part One	5/1/84
6L		Part Two	6/1/84
6L		Part Three	12/1/84
6L		Part Four	13/1/84
6M	**The Awakening**	Part One	19/1/84
6M		Part Two	20/1/84
6N	**Frontios**	Part One	26/1/84
6N		Part Two	27/1/84
6N		Part Three	2/2/84
6N		Part Four	3/2/84
6P	**Resurrection of the Daleks**	Part One	8/2/84
6P		Part Two	15/2/84
6Q	**Planet of Fire**	Part One	23/2/84
6Q		Part Two	24/2/84
6Q		Part Three	1/3/84
6Q		Part Four	2/3/84
6R	**The Caves of Androzani**	Part One	8/3/84
6R		Part Two	9/3/84
6R		Part Three	15/3/84
6R		Part Four	16/3/84
6S	**The Twin Dilemma**	Part One	22/3/84
6S		Part Two	23/3/84
6S		Part Three	29/3/84

6S		Part Four	30/3/84

6T	**Attack of the Cybermen**	Part One	5/1/85
6T		Part Two	12/1/85
6V	**Vengeance on Varos**	Part One	19/1/85
6V		Part Two	26/1/85
6X	**The Mark of the Rani**	Part One	2/2/85
6X		Part Two	9/2/85
6W	**The Two Doctors**	Part One	16/2/85
6W		Part Two	23/2/85
6W		Part Three	2/3/85
6Y	**Timelash**	Part One	9/3/85
6Y		Part Two	16/3/85
6Z	**Revelation of the Daleks**	Part One	23/3/85
6Z		Part Two	30/3/85

*(**Slipback** – six part radio-play, 25/7/85 to 8/8/85)*

Season 23

7A	**The Trial of a Time Lord**	Part One	6/9/86
7A		Part Two	13/9/86
7A		Part Three	20/9/86
7A		Part Four	27/9/86
7B		Part Five	4/10/86
7B		Part Six	11/10/86
7B		Part Seven	18/10/86
7B		Part Eight	25/10/86
7C		Part Nine	1/11/86
7C		Part Ten	8/11/86
7C		Part Eleven	15/11/86
7C		Part Twelve	22/11/86
7C		Part Thirteen	29/11/86
7C		Part Fourteen	6/12/86

Season 24

7D	**Time and the Rani**	Part One	7/9/87
7D		Part Two	14/9/87
7D		Part Three	21/9/87
7D		Part Four	28/9/87
7E	**Paradise Towers**	Part One	5/10/87
7E		Part Two	12/10/87
7E		Part Three	19/10/87
7E		Part Four	26/10/87
7F	**Delta and the Bannermen**	Part One	2/11/87
7F		Part Two	9/11/87
7F		Part Three	16/11/87

7G	**Dragonfire**	Part One	23/11/87
7G		Part Two	30/11/87
7G		Part Three	7/12/87

Season 25

7H	**Remembrance of the Daleks**	Part One	5/10/88
7H		Part Two	12/10/88
7H		Part Three	19/10/88
7H		Part Four	26/10/88
7L	**The Happiness Patrol**	Part One	2/11/88
7L		Part Two	9/11/88
7L		Part Three	16/11/88
7K	**Silver Nemesis**	Part One	23/11/88
7K		Part Two	30/11/88
7K		Part Three	7/12/88
7J	**The Greatest Show in the Galaxy**	Part One	14/12/88
7J		Part Two	21/12/88
7J		Part Three	28/12/88
7J		Part Four	4/1/89

Season 26

7N	**Battlefield**	Part One	6/9/89
7N		Part Two	13/9/89
7N		Part Three	20/9/89
7N		Part Four	27/9/89
7Q	**Ghost Light**	Part One	4/10/89
7Q		Part Two	11/10/89
7Q		Part Three	18/10/89
7M	**The Curse of Fenric**	Part One	25/10/89
7M		Part Two	1/11/89
7M		Part Three	8/11/89
7M		Part Four	15/11/89
7P	**Survival**	Part One	22/11/89
7P		Part Two	29/11/89
7P		Part Three	6/12/89

*(**Paradise of Death** – five part radio play, 27/8/93 to 24/9/93)*
*(**Dimensions in Time** – two parts, 27-28/11/93 in Children in Need/Noel's House Party)*
*(**The Ghosts of N-Space** – six part radio play, 20/1/96 to 24/2/96)*

Doctor Who: The Movie   27/5/96

*(NB All transmission dates are first UK network transmission. **The Five Doctors** and **Doctor Who: The Movie** were first broadcast in the USA. In the UK, some transmissions were on a different day in Wales.)*

THE DOCTORS

🎯 **William Hartnell**
> *100,000 BC* to *The Tenth Planet*, plus *The Three Doctors* (role of the First Doctor played by Richard Hurndall in *The Five Doctors*, and by Peter Cushing in the two cinema films, *Dr. Who and the Daleks* and *Daleks: Invasion Earth 2150 AD*).

🎯 **Patrick Troughton**
> *The Power of the Daleks* to *The War Games*, plus *The Three Doctors*, *The Five Doctors* and *The Two Doctors* (and uncredited introductory appearance in *The Tenth Planet*).

🎯 **Jon Pertwee**
> *Spearhead from Space* to *Planet of the Spiders*, plus *The Five Doctors* (and *Paradise of Death* and *The Ghosts of N-Space* on radio).

🎯 **Tom Baker**
> *Robot* to *Logopolis* (with uncredited introductory appearance in *Planet of the Spiders*).

🎯 **Peter Davison**
> *Castrovalva* to *The Caves of Androzani* (with credited introductory appearance in *Logopolis*).

🎯 **Colin Baker**
> *The Twin Dilemma* to *The Trial of a Time Lord* (with credited introductory appearance in *The Caves of Androzani*).

🎯 **Sylvester McCoy**
> *Time and the Rani* to *Survival* (plus substantial appearance in *Doctor Who: The Movie*).

🎯 **Paul McGann**
> *Doctor Who: The Movie*.

THE COMPANIONS

Susan Foreman (Carole Ann Ford) – **100,000 BC** to **The Dalek Invasion of Earth,** plus **The Five Doctors.**

Ian Chesterton (William Russell) – **100,000 BC** to **The Chase.**

Barbara Wright (Jacqueline Hill) – **100,000 BC** to **The Chase.**

Vicki (Maureen O'Brien) – **The Rescue** to **The Myth Makers.**

Steven Taylor (Peter Purves) – **The Chase** to **The Savages.**

Katarina (Adrienne Hill) – **The Myth Makers** to **The Daleks' Master Plan.**

Sara Kingdom (Jean Marsh) – **The Daleks' Master Plan.**

Dodo Chaplet (Jackie Lane) – **The Massacre of St. Bartholomew's Eve** to **The War Machines.**

Ben Jackson (Michael Craze) – **The War Machines** to **The Faceless Ones.**

Polly (Anneke Wills) – **The War Machines** to **The Faceless Ones.**

Jamie McCrimmon (Fraser Hines) – **The Highlanders** to **The War Games,** plus **The Two Doctors** (and **The Five Doctors,** as a 'projection').

Victoria Waterfield (Deborah Watling) – **The Evil of the Daleks** to **Fury from the Deep** (with credited valedictory appearance in **The Wheel in Space**).

Zoe Herriot (Wendy Padbury) – **The Wheel in Space** to **The War Games** (and **The Five Doctors,** as a 'projection').

Colonel/Brigadier Alistair Gordon Lethbridge-Stewart (Nicholas Courtney) – **The Web of Fear, The Invasion, Spearhead from Space** to **Day of the Daleks, The Time Monster** to **The Three Doctors, The Green Death** to **Invasion of the Dinosaurs, Planet of the Spiders** to **Robot, Terror of the Zygons, Mawdryn Undead, The Five Doctors, Battlefield.**

Corporal/Sergeant/RSM Benton (John Levene) – **The Invasion, The Ambassadors of Death** to **The Claws of Axos, The Daemons** to **Day of the Daleks, The Time Monster** to **The Three Doctors, The Green Death, Invasion of the Dinosaurs, Planet of the Spiders** to

Robot, Terror of the Zygons, The Android Invasion.

Liz Shaw (Caroline John) – **Spearhead from Space** to **Inferno** (and **The Five Doctors**, as a 'projection').

Jo Grant (Katy Manning) – **Terror of the Autons** to **The Green Death**.

Captain Mike Yates (Richard Franklin) – **Terror of the Autons** to **The Claws of Axos**, **The Daemons** to **Day of the Daleks**, **The Time Monster**, **The Green Death**, **Invasion of the Dinosaurs**, **Planet of the Spiders** (by then no longer in the army) (plus **The Five Doctors** as a 'projection').

Sarah Jane Smith (Elisabeth Sladen) – **The Time Warrior** to **The Hand of Fear**, plus **The Five Doctors** (and **K9 and Company: A Girl's Best Friend, Paradise of Death** and **The Ghosts of N-Space**).

Harry Sullivan (Ian Marter) – **Robot** to **Terror of the Zygons**, plus **The Android Invasion**.

Leela (Louise Jameson) – **The Face of Evil** to **The Invasion of Time**.

K9 (voice by John Leeson/David Brierley) – **The Invisible Enemy** to **Warriors' Gate**, plus **The Five Doctors** (and **K9 and Company: A Girl's Best Friend**).

Romana (1st incarnation) (Mary Tamm) – **The Ribos Operation** to **The Armageddon Factor**.

Romana (2nd incarnation) (Lalla Ward) – **Destiny of the Daleks** to **Warriors' Gate**.

Adric (Matthew Waterhouse) – **Full Circle** to **Earthshock** (plus **Time-Flight** as a 'projection' and **The Caves of Androzani** as a 'memory').

Nyssa (Sarah Sutton) – **The Keeper of Traken** to **Terminus** (plus **The Caves of Androzani** as a 'memory').

Tegan Jovanka (Janet Fielding) – **Logopolis** to **Resurrection of the Daleks** (plus **The Caves of Androzani** as a 'memory').

Vislor Turlough (Mark Strickson) – **Mawdryn Undead** to **Planet of Fire** (plus **The Caves of Androzani** as a 'memory').

Peri Brown (Nicola Bryant) – **Planet of Fire** to **The Trial of a Time Lord** (parts five to eight).

- Melanie Bush (Bonnie Langford) – **The Trial of a Time Lord** (parts nine to fourteen) to **Dragonfire**.

- Ace (Sophie Aldred) – **Dragonfire** to **Survival**.

- Dr Grace Holloway (Daphne Ashbrook) – **Doctor Who: The Movie**.